INDIA
CONTEMPORARY
DESIGN

INDIA
CONTEMPORARY
DESIGN

Fashion | Graphics | Interiors

Divia Patel

Lustre Press
Roli Books
in association with
V&A Publishing
London

DEDICATION

For my creative and
inspiring mother,
Shushila.

Detail from Smoke House Deli interior,
Phoenix Mills, Mumbai.
Designed by The Busride Design Studio, 2011.
Photo courtesy The Busride Design Studio.

Acknowledgments

I thank my colleagues at the V&A for their encouragement and advice: Glenn Adamson, Anjali Bulley, Mark Eastman, Christine Guth, Liz Miller, and to Richard Davis and Jaron James for the V&A photography. My departmental colleagues for their particular support: Anna Jackson, Nick Barnard, Rosemary Crill, and Susan Stronge. For their expertise and companionship when travelling in India, I thank Oriole Cullen, Jana Scholze, Abraham Thomas, and especially Orla Houston-Jibo. I am grateful to Ruchita Madhok, Ana Pavia, Liz Stanford, and Shirely Surya for their assistance with research.

In India, to those who extended their hospitality and friendship and made my visits pleasurable and productive: Poulomi Das and Priyam Chatterjee, Ruth Gee, the Godrej family, Mike Knowles, Adam Puskin, Manju Rajan, Kavita Singh, Mayank Man Singh, Parmesh Shahani, Aanchal Sodhani, and Divya Thakur. Thanks also to colleagues at the National Institute of Design: Professor Pradyumna Vyas and Tanishka Kachru.

I could not have completed this book without the designers and design studios that gave me their time, hospitality, and their generosity with images:

Fashion: David Abraham, Amit Aggarwal, Aneeth Arora, Deepak Bagwani, Paromita Banerjee, Nachiket Barve, Samat Chauhan, Shilpa Chavan, Kallol Datta, Rimzim Dadu, Sanjay Garg, Masaba Gupta, Gaurav Jai Gupta, Swati Khalsi, Anamika Khanna, Priya Kishore, Nida Mahmood, Rahul Mishra, Payal Mukherjee, Shenali Sema, Rajiv Sethi and his team at Asian Heritage Foundation, Small Shop (Jason and Anshu), Rajesh Pratap Singh, Kiran Uttam Ghosh.

Graphics: S. Anand, Rajesh Dahiya, Himanshu Dogra, Aman Khanna, Lokesh Karekar, Ishan Khosla, Tania Khosla, Sameer Kulavoor, Hanif Kureshi, Tejas Mangeshkar, Rathna Ramanathan, Kurnal Rawat, Akila

Seshasayee, V. Sunil and his team at Motherland, Divya Thakur, H. Kumar Vyas.

Interiors: Maithili Ahluwalia, Ayaz Basrai, Charles Correa, Siddhartha Das, Nipa Doshi and Jonathan Levien, Vikram Goyal, Gunjan Gupta, Kapil Gupta, Bijoy and Priya Jain, Ayush and Geetanjali Kasliwal, Sandeep Khosla, Andrea Noronha, Satyendra Pakhale, Jigisha Patel, Anupam Poddar, Mann Singh, MP Ranjan, Rebecca Reubens, Rajiv Saini, Sanjeev Sangaru, Sahil (Bagga) and Sarthak (Sengupta), Mann Singh.

This manuscript has benefited from the comments of several readers to whom I am most grateful: David Abraham, Glenn Adamson, Suchitra Balasubramanian, Rosemary Crill, Oriole Cullen, Rathna Ramanathan, Jana Scholze, and Laila Tyabji. I thank Graham Parlett for his assistance with the editing.

I am thankful to Priya Kapoor, Neelam Narula, Saloni Vaid, Bonita Vaz-Shimray, and Neharika Gupta from Roli Books for seeing the value of this book and making it happen.

As ever, gratitude goes to my family and friends for keeping me grounded, but most of all, for his constant encouragement, advice and nourishment, and for just being beside me, I am indebted to my partner, Jonathan.

7

CONTENTS

Rangoli Headpiece.
Designed by Little Shilpa, 2006.
Photo courtesy Little Shilpa and Suresh Natarajan.

INTRODUCTION

INDIA 2000

Between 2000 and 2010 India's economic and political ascendancy were relentlessly charted in the world press. The national growth rate of 8 per cent, the rise of the middle classes, increased consumer spending were all markers of success resulting from the liberalization of the economy in the 1990s.[1] Many of these press reports also underlined the necessity for India to find solutions to relieve inequality and poverty but, after a long period of stagnation, these sparks of activity were perceived as having put the country on the path to much needed change.

Visible expressions of India's growth appeared in the form of rapid urban expansion and consumerist middle-class lifestyles epitomized by gated communities and shopping malls.[2] Within the metropolitan cities of Mumbai, Delhi, Kolkata, and Bengaluru one of the manifestations of this success was seen in the sprouting of stylish new boutiques, designer shops, smart new restaurants, and dynamic art gallery spaces. For certain spectrums of society, these changes reflected an increased sense of confidence, aspiration and pride in being Indian.

This book focuses on the metropolitan cities and the response of the design community to India's changing environment. It documents fashion, graphic and interior design as symbols of the post-liberalization creative awakening. The designers under consideration here are mainly those who have begun practising between 2000 and 2013, although there are a few exceptions. An over-arching theme is the way in which they define their work and negotiate identity and Indian-ness in a contemporary global context. Emerging from this study is a picture of multiplicity, one which explores the exchange of ideas and the networks of connections between people and places that are at the heart of creativity within these three fields.

Facing page:
Interior of Indigo Deli,
Colaba, Mumbai.
Designed by
Samira Rathod, 2007.
Photo courtesy Roli Collection.

Following pages:
Interior of Rajesh Pratap Singh's
retail space, Lodi Colony,
New Delhi.
Designed by Rajesh Pratap
Singh and assisted by Amit
Chhabra of Livin' Colors, 2006.
Photo courtesy Tarun Khiwal.

MODERNISM, MODERNITY AND NATIONAL IDENTITY

India's plurality is one of its defining features: regional, religious and linguistic identities existed long before any form of national identity. The colonial importation of anthropological and archaeological practices along with the implementation of systems of surveying, documenting and mapping the subcontinent served to classify its diversity but also began the process of assembling India as a complete entity in the 19th century.[3] The need for a unifying identity for India came with the nationalist movement and the desire for an independent nation state. Jawaharlal Nehru, India's first prime minister, emphasized the notion of 'unity in diversity' and cultural mixing, along with a grand historical past that could lead to a strong nation state for the future. Nehru constructed an 'idea of India' where complex history and cultural diversity were at the heart of a society that he saw as a series of interconnected differences, and where Indian-ness was 'layered, adjustable, imagined', not fixed.[4] For him, a modern Indian identity could only emerge out of the institutional

The Legislative Assembly building, Chandigarh. Designed by Le Corbusier, 1951. Photo courtesy Alamy.

14

framework of a democratic state which would also enable India to be part of the wider world.

Nehru had a vision for India which saw it as a progressive, industrialized, secular and socialist state, claiming a prominent position within the international arena. He began large-scale industrialization through nationalized projects that saw the construction of factories and dams. Investment in science and technology were seen as a means of progressing beyond the confines of tradition and the shackles of poverty. This vision of a modern, technology-led nation, one that inspired a national identity, was articulated symbolically through architecture. After Independence, the partition of India and the creation of Pakistan meant that the state of Punjab was split between the two with the capital city of Lahore located in Pakistan. The need for a new state capital for India's portion of the Punjab was embraced by Nehru who suggested looking to the West for suitable town planners and architects. The Swiss/French architect Charles-Édouard Jeanneret (Le Corbusier) was invited by the Punjab state administrators in 1951 as the architectural advisor for the city. As a pioneer of the modern movement in Europe, his design and architecture would project the modernity that Nehru aspired to.

Modernist architecture emphasized functionality and a negation of ornamentation and traditional styles. The simple, clean, efficient, abstract forms encouraged by the movement alongside the use of metal, concrete, and new construction technologies enabled a universal response to those post-war nations seeking to rebuild their towns and cities. Modernism was a symbol of future opportunities for India; it was the spirit of modernist thinking, the social aspect of modernism that Nehru found most compelling. The building of infrastructure, hospitals, schools, and housing projects was part of this.[5] In a rare speech on architecture given in 1959, Nehru stated that 'what I like above all is the creative approach, not being tied down to what has been done by our forefathers and the like, but thinking out in new terms, to think in terms of light and air and ground and water and human beings, not in terms of rules and regulations laid down by our ancestors.'[6] Chandigarh's Capital Complex, which consisted of the Secretariat, the Assembly, and the High Court, was completed in 1960. However, despite being a symbolic representation of India's progressive and liberal aspirations for the Nehruvian state, the universalism of modernist architecture was later

criticized for its disdain for local conditions and its alienating segregation of public and private spaces.[7]

Beyond Chandigarh, modernism made an impact in Delhi and Ahmedabad.[8] Architects such as Achyut Kanvinde, Balkrishna Doshi, and Charles Correa, who were trained in the West, tried to adapt modernism to the Indian environment. Kanvinde believed passionately that architecture should be an expression of its time, with science and technology at the heart of a universal language of architecture, he successfully convinced Nehru against the implementation of an official national style of architecture based on traditional motifs, which was being proposed after Independence.[9] This was echoed by Nehru in his speech of March 1959: 'The past was good when it was the present, but you cannot bring it forward when the world has changed into a technological period.'[10]

Modernism as a movement and modernity as a process negotiated through art and culture were explored and promoted in the pages of the journal *MARG*. Following the London based group, *MARS*, which aimed to support and promote British modernism, the Modern Architecture Research Group (MARG) brought together a few progressive architects with the object of stimulating a popular interest in the appreciation of architecture in India. The founder and editor, Mulk Raj Anand, aimed to cover a much broader field encompassing arts and crafts, industrial design, painting and sculpture, alongside architecture. The journal, the first of its kind, strove to mould an Indian modernity for the early decades of Independence with articles on urban planning and architecture featuring Le Corbusier and Frank Lloyd Wright, thus projecting a sense of internationalism that echoed the Nehruvian view of progress. The artists profiled within were of the modern movement; from Amrita Sher-Gil, Jamini Roy, and George Keyts to M.F. Husain and Raza of the Progressive Artists Group, they explored a broader internationalism in their paintings than the narrow nationalism of previous art movements.[11] Appealing to and only affordable by urban educated élite, the magazine's 'role was activist, raising consciousness and giving people tools to live a better life'.[12]

Modernity was also expressed through the advertisements placed in *MARG*; in the immediate aftermath of Independence, companies were eager to show their contribution to the building of the nation.

Facing page:
Advertisement for Tata
Enterprises, 1953-4.
Published in MARG, vol.VII/iii.
Photo courtesy
V&A Museum, London.

17

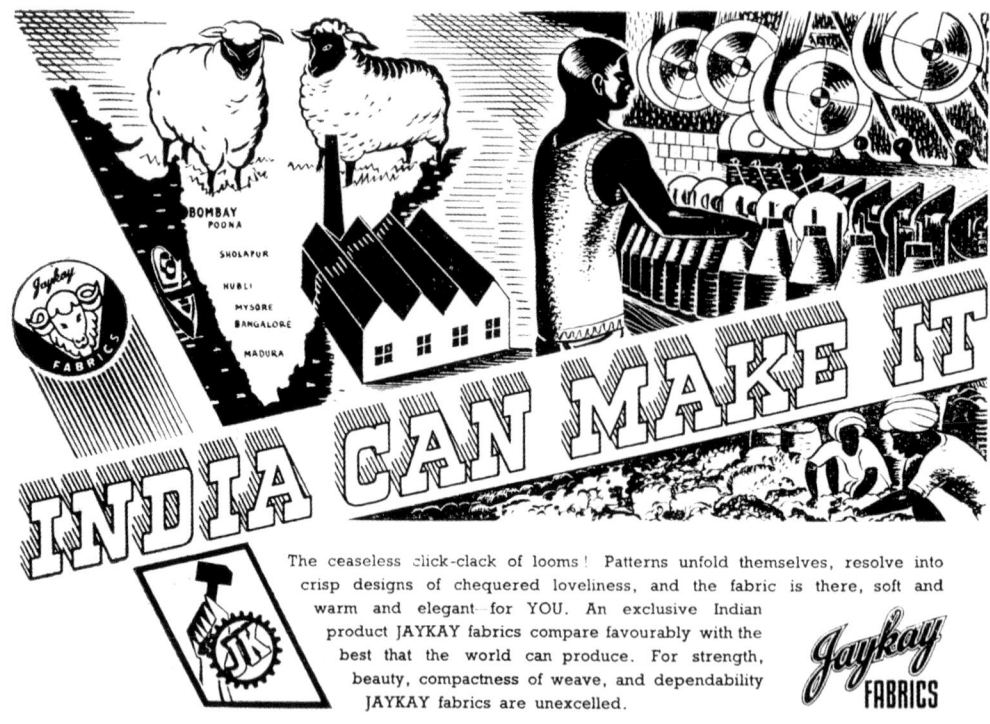

INDIA CAN MAKE IT

The ceaseless click-clack of looms! Patterns unfold themselves, resolve into crisp designs of chequered loveliness, and the fabric is there, soft and warm and elegant for YOU. An exclusive Indian product JAYKAY fabrics compare favourably with the best that the world can produce. For strength, beauty, compactness of weave, and dependability JAYKAY fabrics are unexcelled.

Jaykay FABRICS

THE RAYMOND WOOLLEN MILLS LTD., BOMBAY

Advertisement for Raymond
Mills, 1949-50.
Published in MARG, vol.III/i.
Photo courtesy
V&A Museum, London.

The Cement Marketing Company were constructing everything from wells to villages and towns; Mahindra & Mahindra were equipping the nation for progress through their industrial and agricultural machinery; Raymond Mills, and numerous other mills, were ready to clothe the nation; Godrej were furnishing interiors with their utilitarian designs for homes and offices. However, most impactful was a series of advertisements for Tata Industries. Placed in almost every issue of *MARG* from 1946 to 1956, they conveyed the depth of Tata's engagement with nation-building enterprises. Full-page adverts focused on one theme at a time, from housing to medicine, reassuring the nation of their participation in the most critical roles by proclaiming 'Here, as in all other spheres of reconstruction, Tata steel will play its part.'[13] Emotionally charged narratives informed the people of Tata's generation of electricity to power the nation along with their contribution to India's five year plans to raise standards of living. The accompanying illustrations were unfailingly modern, either in an Art Deco style or another international aesthetic. As a whole they expressed the drive for modernity and the pride that came from a nation reconstructing itself.

TRADITION, CHANGE AND DESIGN

India's progress to full-scale industrialization was going to be a slow process. The immediate and overwhelming need to find solutions for the greater proportion of the population in rural India remained, and it was in this arena that the tensions between tradition and modernity were most acute. During the nationalist movement an alternative form of development had been advocated by Mahatma Gandhi: one of swadeshi or self-sufficiency through small-scale production, as symbolized through khadi, a fabric hand-spun and hand-woven in the villages of India. For him, khadi embodied moral, social, economic and political value. He urged the nation to wear khadi and to spin it. To wear it was to actively and visibly reject imported western textiles which had been flooding India's markets and threatening her own textile industry, and thereby identify oneself politically as a supporter of self-rule. To spin khadi was a means of creating supplementary employment for the masses and he saw craft/village-based economic structures as a more appropriate form of production for Independent India than the full-scale industrialization seen in Europe. Self-reliance was at the heart of Gandhi's teachings and for him village based production was the unifying principle for the formation of an Indian identity.

Gandhi's simplified way of living and his teachings were later cited as useful examples for the contemporary designer. In an exhibition entitled *Design in India*, held at the Commonwealth Institute, London, as part of the festival of India in Britain in 1982, Gandhi was positioned as a 'designer' of the freedom movement whereby his influence gradually and imperceptibly initiated a process of 'redesign' in India's environments at various levels, ranging from open tent-like structures seating a million listeners to a simple pair of sandals; from India's influential communication media to that tiny symbolic machine – the spinning wheel.[14] Gandhi's ashram, his residence from 1917 to 1930, was an example of the austerity with which he surrounded himself and a constant reminder of the 'ideal of simplicity'.[15] Gandhi's simple dhoti, the kurta pyjama or loose shirt and trouser outfit, was 'now universally

accepted for its functionalism, economy and dignity', the re-designed spinning-wheel by Lakshidas Ashar and Gandhi's own re-design of a national cap were part of his legacy to contemporary designers.[16] They spoke of self-reliance, appropriateness, simplicity and a need to engage with, understand, and assist India's masses.

The politicization by Gandhi of khadi, and craft in general, led to its being recognized within the constitution of the newly-independent India. During the following decade this was reflected in the establishment of a series of initiatives all seeking to preserve and promote crafts. This included the All India Handlooms Board of 1952, which sought to develop craft from a national level with apprenticeship programmes and design development centres. The design centres employed some of India's first designers such as Ritin Mazumdar and Shona Ray.[17] In 1956 came the Khadi and Village Industries Commission, the Weavers Service Centres and the Crafts Museum, which were set up to document and create a permanent collection of craft. The Calico Museum was a private initiative set up in 1949 with the same motive but focusing on the textile crafts of India. In 1962, the Handicrafts and Handlooms Export Corporation was created and succeeded through exhibitions and publications to create an export market.[18]

While industrialization was essential to the re-building of the nation, the counter-effects of mass mechanization and mass production were well known. Mulk Raj Anand and others saw the revitalization of the craft communities, particularly the handloom industry, as a means of avoiding 'the suppression of the creative skill of the hand' for the 'routine repetition of the conveyor belt' as experienced by the factory workers of many industrialized countries.[19] Many of the institutions listed above were set up to modernize the handloom industry, to revitalize it and give it a contemporary relevance. While there were structural problems that needed to be addressed, the design debate as voiced through the pages of *MARG* centred on the question of what constituted contemporary design and the placement of tradition within that:

> Tradition means more, it means to understand the national heritage, to know, not only its how, but its why, to feel the spirit of the times and to feel it changing, to build on the old foundations, not merely to repeat them.[20]

Furthermore, in reference to the changing perception of ornamentation in design and in the evolving concept of interior design:

> A contemporary design should make the commodity suitable for contemporary use, in the background of modern life. It should conform with the spirit of the times. These being days when simplicity is preferred to ostentation, the design should be simple and functional... ...Finally, it should conform to other relative factors like architecture, art objects, costumes and furniture of the time to make a homogenous complex.[21]

> Tradition therefore was not to be perceived as static, to be clung to blindly, rather progress required it to be adaptable and open to re-invention, within the spirit of the time to meet the "contemporary challenges of new functions, new technologies, new environment, and new relationships".[22]

The meaning of design in a newly-independent nation, seeking to modernize, yet whose lifestyle still drew substantially from ancient cultural traditions, was soon to be addressed in a new institution set up by Nehru. In 1958, on the advice of Pupul Jayakar, Nehru invited the American designers Charles and Ray Eames to India.[23] They were asked to recommend a design-led training programme to aid small-industries. The result of their three-month tour across India was *The India Report*, a paper which recommended 'an institute of design, research and service which would also be an advanced training medium.' *The India Report* was a key reference point for the founding faculty and has become part of its design pedagogy, with its contemporary relevance often cited.

The objective of the new design institute was 'to create an alert and impatient national conscience – a conscience concerned with the quality and ultimate values of the environment'. The report warned that India's advantage in the face of such rapid changes brought on by the process of modernity was her knowledge of the destructive forces of capitalism on tradition, and the chance to avoid making the same mistake as other nations in their transition. It urged an exploration, starting from the village level, of the ideals that Indian people value for a good life and to study the problems of the environment and shelter. In their de-construction of the design of an Indian water pot, the lota, charting its evolution to a perfect utilitarian and aesthetic form, the Eameses highlighted the importance of the evolutionary process of design that was inherent in India's traditional production. To respond to modern India's needs

22

in an appropriate way, the *Eames Report* hoped that the new design institute could cultivate a sympathetic working ethos which would 'appraise and solve the problems of our coming times with the same tremendous service, dignity and love that the lota served its time'.[24] Thus, design solutions required sensitization to the environment and the people, and change should be a conscious process related to evolving needs. *The India Report* therefore, rather than implement a system of non-contextual modernization, reinforced some of the traditional associations of design being integral to crafts and everyday living, distancing itself from the colonial distinction between the 'fine arts' and crafts.[25] It was also to introduce a new understanding of industrial design and design education. However, while the significance of the report should not be undermined, the constant citing of its relevance today also brings with it the danger of over-romanticization and simplification of the contemporary environment.

The new institute was initially to be located in Bangalore (now Bengaluru). However, proactive intervention by the visionary textile industrialist Gautam Sarabhai led to the founding of the National Institute of Design (NID) in Ahmedabad in 1961. The Sarabhai family were art and science enthusiasts, Gautam's sister, Gira, had trained under the architect Frank Lloyd Wright. Together they called on a small body of people who, like them, had a broad perspective on art, architecture, crafts and the environment. Dashrath Patel and Kumar Vyas were two of the first faculty members. Vyas had been trained in the West and was sent to Ulm School of Design in Germany to observe their product design programme in order to begin a faculty training programme. Other training programmes focused on textile design, furniture, and ceramics. Dashrath Patel was sent out on a world tour to study and make international contacts. It took twelve years to develop the faculty, with the first students being admitted in 1972.[26] With faculty members trained outside of India and familiar with the teachings of the Bauhaus as well as the Ulm School of Design, and with an ongoing stream of international art and design professionals on exchange programmes, the institute was aware of the need to think modern within an Indian context.

In teaching the value of design, Vyas explored the Indian notion of *Kalaa;* traditional design thinking is rooted in this concept which suggests unity among all human arts, skills, sciences, and techniques. The sense of universality and integration inherent in this term lasted until the European concepts of art and craft were brought to India. Schools of Art were set up in Calcutta (now Kolkata), Bombay (now Mumbai), Madras (now Chennai), and Lahore to impart a British system of design education which saw arts and crafts as distinct entities separated from day-to-day living. This separation from daily life, which was also a result of urbanization and industrialization, had major implications for design becoming a separate function from craft/art production. Vyas drew a distinction between the 'learned' process of design, a response to industrialization whereby a trained designer takes a deliberate and methodical approach to a problem, and the 'evolutionary' process of design, which is unstructured, organic, collectively produced by anonymous individuals representing several generations.[27] By drawing students' attention to the evolutionary heritage represented by India's living craft traditions, Vyas and his colleagues at NID hoped they would learn from the past to develop the future. In doing so, they felt that their designs would be appropriate to the Indian context in all its dimensions: physical, psychological, and socio-cultural. NID's engagement with craft communities developed into programmes of field research and documentation of existing traditions with the aim of preserving knowledge and sourcing new avenues of income generation that had the potential to raise these communities out of poverty. Student designers were taught to apply contemporary knowledge of markets to craft production, marrying existing rural traditions with contemporary urban needs. Alongside these initiatives and in recognition of the importance of industrial design, the government set up the Industrial Design Centre (IDC) in 1969 as part of the Indian Institute of Technology (IIT) in Bombay. NID and IDC aimed to produce professionals that could make an impact on national development.

Despite the optimism that attended the school's founding, there were significant challenges to face. The first students graduating from NID in the mid-1970s were faced with an industry that had no understanding of the purpose of designers. India had a protected market from imports; designers were expected to enter industry to 'copy' with most companies licensing foreign designs. This did little to encourage innovation or foster an entrepreneurial competitiveness. There is very little documentation about the design industry during this period; however, one aspect which is often written about is the focus on grassroots activities. The 1970s are projected as a time of idealism in which designers were involved with community development projects;

24

the Jawaja leather-craft programme being the most successful in terms of design intervention leading to the re-vitalization of a village economy. International recognition of such grassroots projects was channelled into the first-ever UN conference on design for development held at the NID in 1979. The aspirations of the conference in its desire to create a more equal world remained an ideal, as the focus for design began to shift in the 1980s and 90s. Liberalization and globalization saw the gradual opening up of the markets, with global and domestic competitiveness beginning to promote the need for design and designers in the corporate sector and beyond.[28]

Today, a debate continues about the appropriate definition of design in India, which still seeks a balance between modernity and tradition. In the stereotypical modernist conception of design in the West, the discipline has been documented as a linear progression which focuses on and thereby elevates the status of individual designers. Early western design historians fixed on design as a product of industry, mass produced and machine made. This implies that design started with mass production and is limited to areas where it is part of an industrial economic system. It also denies that 'design' existed before the 1950s or indeed that it can exist in pre-modern societies. India's industrial revolution came almost a century later than in the West and it did not industrialize fully, leaving the coexistence of agrarian and modern societies.

A wider definition of design, which I have adopted in this study, includes practices that have developed out of mixed economies, in which industrial and agrarian coexist.[29] This, in turn, implies that an alternative definition of modernity is required, one that allows for such complexities. Modernity should not be regarded as monolithic. There are many modernities – old, new, and incomplete.[30] Correspondingly, there are many structures of tradition.[31] To think of tradition as an invariable and rigid entity is misleading for it can be re-invented and re-evaluated in different contexts.[32] The Sanskrit word *parampara* provides a more appropriate and flexible understanding; often equated with tradition, it translates as 'one following the other or proceeding from one to the other'.[33] Kapila Vatsyayan has described it as 'a double-reed flute. One reed is a perennial strain, a tonic, immutable trans-space and –time; the other reed plays the tune of immediate time and space. The one is repetitive but stable; the other changing. The two together create the music that sounds different at different times.'[34]

Advertisement for India Poised campaign by Times of India Group, 2007, New Delhi. Photo courtesy Divia Patel.

LIBERALIZATION, GLOBALIZATION AND NATIONAL IDENTITY

On the 60th anniversary of India's independence, the *Times of India* group ran a campaign called *India Poised*; the television adverts were emotive and empowering. One of them stated:

> 1857 India awakens. 1947 Freedom. 1991 The economy unleashed. 2007 The year of India?

> The world's spotlights are focused on India. Our achievers are being appointed to the helm of the world's leading multinational companies, and our companies are getting ready to take over global players many times their size.

> The world's attention feels good. But we know in our hearts that we still have a long way to go.

The *India Poised* campaign reflected the spirit of optimism and aspiration that was felt by a growing urban middle class, that their

Infosys S.D.B. Park 6,
Bengaluru.
Designed by
Hafeez Contractor, 2007.
Photo courtesy Infosys Limited.

nation was experiencing a re-birth after the stagnation of the 1970-80s. It echoed the spirit of the post-independence nation-building period. Liberalization was seen to be responsible for India becoming the fourth largest economy and the resulting armies of 2.5 million ambitious graduates, strong foreign investment, and globally responsive companies being at the centre of its ascendancy.[35] The impact of these changes has led to a host of writing about the opening up of the economy, the new middle class, and notions of identity and Indian-ness both at an academic and popular level.[36]

With liberalization came the forces of globalization. Historically India has, as a geographical, political, and cultural entity, been interacting with the outside world, where as the contemporary phase of globalization is 'the coming together of a particular set of processes, technological, economic, social, political, environmental, and cultural which today demonstrates an unprecedented level of interconnectedness'.[37] These processes are noticeable through the proliferation of mass media, financial networks, people and their migration, ideas and concepts; they can be regional, global or transnational and at different levels of intensity and velocity.[38]

One of the most visual manifestations of India's globalization is through architecture and particularly the glass and steel buildings spreading across the urban landscape. Their sleek, shiny exteriors and their emulation of high-concept designs from around the world represent the global culture of commerce, the flow of money, multinational corporations, and market opportunities across national boundaries. Most symbolic of this are the offices and campus sites designed by the architect Hafeez Contractor for Infosys, India's leading global consulting and IT services supplier. In Bengaluru, Hyderabad, and Pune their offices stand in stark contrast to the surrounding environment, their forms and facades proudly proclaiming alignment to a universal aesthetic which represents the technology of the age and their allegiance to a universal way of working, living, and consuming. They stand for commerce and global capital.[39] For other architects, the broader design community, those concerned about the environment, these buildings spark fear because of their homogenizing tendencies, their lack of appropriateness to local contexts and Indian environmental conditions. Furthermore, the associated cultures of these buildings promote western lifestyles and are perceived to dominate and erode national cultures and local traditions. However, a characteristic of India's past history has been 'its capacity to assimilate, absorb and accommodate cultural diversities drawn from a variety of sources, and to form a loosely integrated unity with considerable autonomy of the constituent elements. This underlying process has been named as syncretism – an accommodation of new elements without rejecting the old.'[40] Today, local or national cultures absorb and adapt to global cultural forms rather than get subsumed by them; global forms get contextualized into local environments, as much as vice versa. This process of 'glocalization' is a two-way process; the global and local in this contemporary scenario interpenetrate and continue to create a syncretic mix.[41]

DESIGN CULTURES: GLOBAL, LOCAL, COSMOPOLITAN

This book explores the design culture of spaces within the metropolitan cities of India that have emerged from this era of liberalization and globalization. It focuses on the creativeness of designers who work with graphics, interiors and fashion and show how they have responded to the changing environment in a multitude of creative ways. Their responsiveness is reflective of their cosmopolitanism;

their increased awareness of the world, their intercultural contact and interconnectedness which is driven by their education, travel, and exposure through technological media. They are part of globalizing cities where their communication with the world is more acute. Cosmopolitanism, because it relates an individual to the wider world, is also a way of seeing oneself, of constructing an identity in relation to a range of other cultures and traditions. It does not imply a discarding of national consciousness, for the idea of the nation-state maintains a strong emotional bond. Rather, cosmopolitanism implies multiple identities including a national identity. In today's global environment, identity is flexible and fluid.[42]

Focusing on designers who are creating an Indian cosmopolitan identity, this book is concerned mainly with the production of their work and the ideas and influences that shape them. The circulation and consumption of their work requires more ethnographic-driven research, although a fair generalization of the consumers of these products would be an upwardly mobile, affluent, young, creative, cosmopolitan group. One aspect of this circulation and consumption which helps to frame the studies in this book needs mentioning here and is based on Guy Julier's analysis of the 'culture of design': That is an exploration of the spaces in which design has been 'intensified', one in which there is a concentration of design-focused activity.[43] The evolution of a design milieu in the Colaba area of South Mumbai and Hauz Khas village, Delhi are presented here as examples. Both areas have long histories of creative enterprise, but in the period of our study, emerging businesses suggest the 'intensification' of a design culture.[44] In Colaba the rise of boutique shops that sell fashion, graphics and interior products is evident. Stores such as Bungalow 8 set up in its current location in 2005 by Maithili Ahluwalia, Bombay Electric in 2006 by Priya Kishore, and Design Temple in 2010 by Divya Thakur, project a local-global message through their design philosophies, products, and retail spaces. Contemporary art galleries such as Chatterjee and Lal, restaurants like Indigo deli, and booksellers like Art and Design Bookstore, add to this dynamic environment. Hauz Khas village is more experimental but you will find boutiques, restaurants, and design studios such as Nappa Dori, The Living Room, and Ishan Khosla Design based here. These environments cater for a 'designed' lifestyle, they encourage the appreciation of design through their products and the experiences they offer, and they promote the desire for more of the same. Design magazines, websites and blogging speed-up the transfer of information and contribute to this reflexive cycle.

These spaces reflect a certain design philosophy. Maithili Ahluwalia, Priya Kishore and Divya Thakur, are all post-liberalization children who have travelled, worked or lived outside of India. They have all stressed the importance of not mimicking the West but of being part of a more global design dialogue that celebrates an understanding of the local. They and the other designers discussed here locate an aesthetic and ideological Indian-ness in numerous traditions: For some it is to be found within the villages of India, for others it is in the splendour of India's palaces and for others still, it is present on the streets, in the everyday elements that constitute popular culture.[45] Tradition/s is the bearer of authenticity and is used to confer a cultural identity into their work. In this book tradition=*parampara* as it acknowledges a progressive movement that captures the responsiveness of the design community to a changing contemporary context.

Any one study cannot, of course, claim to be a comprehensive account of India's enormous design landscape. In my role as a curator at the Victoria and Albert Museum, London, the remit to collect and document contemporary design from India instigated this investigation. Research revealed a significant amount of activity in the subject areas of fashion, graphics, interiors, and design for India's less advantaged groups. The rise of Systems Design and innovation for and from the 'bottom-of-the-pyramid' has received considerable documentation through a number of publications which preserves their contribution to the history of design in India.[46] However, there is a distinct lack of written material with regard to the other three areas in comparison to their counterparts in the West. Within the design community itself, the obligation to design for the whole population has led to self-criticism: dissatisfaction with the current emphasis on style over substance, form over function and aesthetics over innovation. However, as history has shown, design in all its disciplines is a reflection of society and as such if the study of design history in India, in years to come, is to be reflective of the whole, then all aspects of design need to be documented. This book therefore, is a small stepping stone in bridging that lacuna of knowledge. It documents the shaping of a cosmopolitan environment through fashion, graphics, and interiors between the period of 2000 and 2013, a moment of fervent activity.

While researching and writing this book during 2010-13, there has been a rise in platforms for the promotion of design at a variety of levels and for different audiences: The India Design Forum, launched by the Coimbatore Centre for Contemporary Art in 2012, India Design 2012 initiated by Ogaan and Elle Décor, the Unbox Festival organized by the British Council, join the well-established Kyoorius Design Yatra launched in 2005 by Rajesh Kejriwal.[47] Generating knowledge in the field, is the rise of blogs and websites, which allow for an immediacy in information transition; noteworthy examples include Indian By Design launched by Kavita Rayirath in 2008, Design for India run by Professor M.P. Ranjan, Designwala by Shagun Singh and Richard Lin in 2009, Designdesh by A. Balasubramaniam started in 2011, Vision First started in 2011 by a team of ten design thinkers, and Perch on the Web set up by Ruchita Madhok and Aditya Palsule in 2012. However, very much a sign of the times and typical of the nature of the medium, these sites are prone to decline or disappear as fast as they have arisen. Magazines in all three fields are noted in the individual chapters. On a governmental level, the National Design Policy was issued in February 2007 with a vision to have a 'design enabled Indian industry, which can impact both the national economy and the quality of life in a positive manner.' With promised upgrading of design institutions, the setting up of specialized Design centres and the creation of the India Design Council in 2009, there is potential for design to be integrated into 'economic, industrial and societal development and in improving quality of products and services'.[48] However, underlying this burst of design-related activity, there is financial crisis and economic uncertainty spreading across the globe, and many reports are talking of the harsh realities behind the gloss of India's success story. How this decline affects the new-found interest in design and the designers as represented in this book remains to be seen. In the face of continuous and unpredictable change, this book is an attempt to capture the zeitgeist of a brief moment in India's design history.

31

FASHION in INDIA

Fashion is the most vibrant and visible creative industry in India. Over the period of this study, from 2000 to 2013, the profession has developed to reflect a diversity that incorporates cocktail dresses and beach-wear alongside the draped saris and *ghagra-cholis*. The expansion of the fashion industry is underpinned by the changing economic climate which has made an impact on many levels. Increased affluence has resulted in a growing demand for western fashion brands, many of which have established retail outlets in major cities.[1] Specially designed and targeted products, such as the Hermes Sari collection in 2011 and the Christian Louboutin India shoe range in 2013, help to develop their hold on the Indian consumer. However, the powerful counter-response to this has been the turning-inward of the indigenous fashion industry. Recognizing the strength of their own economy and confident in their creativity, many designers have chosen to focus on an Indian clientele that are becoming more informed about global fashion, rather than pursue western markets or western endorsement as they have in the past. As the forces of liberalization and globalization create new and different environments within India, designers are responding in a myriad of imaginative ways, they produce exciting, rich, innovative clothes, which explore Asian and western aesthetics and forms and draw links between tradition and modernity. They navigate ideas of Indian-ness, and of internationalism with consummate dexterity.

Unlike its western counterpart, Indian fashion is a relatively under-researched field. Meher Castelino's *Fashion Kaleidoscope* published in 1994 represents a singular attempt at documenting fashion from the 1920s to the 1990s exploring catwalk-shows, retails spaces, photography, and print media.[2] In recent years this has been updated within the context of liberalization and emerging markets in *Indian by*

Facing page:
Detail of the interior of Rajesh Pratap Singh's retail space, Emporio Mall, New Delhi. Designed by Lotus, 2008. Photo courtesy Lotus.

33

Interior of Bombay Electric,
Mumbai.
Designed by Priya Kishore, 2006.
Photo courtesy Bombay Electric.

Design: The Pursuit of Luxury and Fashion by Michael Boroian and Alix de Poix, and is complimented by *Powder Room, an insider's guide to the industry* by Shefalee Vasudev.[3] Image-heavy biographies such as *India Fasntastique* by Abu Jani and Sandeep Khosla continue to reinforce the glamour and elitism of the industry.[4] Studies exploring fashion and identity are limited, the exceptions being *Clothing Matters* by Emma Tarlo, *The Sari* by Mukulika Banerjee and Daniel Miller, as well as noteworthy research by Naseem Khan and Dulali Nag.[5]

Indian textiles and dress, by way of contrast, have a strong body of literature recording historical development as well as regional variety in technique and design; these often include elements that slot into a history of fashion.[6] The motivation behind these textile studies is the importance attached to documenting 'tradition'. Fashion, however, is regarded as a reflection of modern consumerist societies and is according to fashion theorists a system defined by constant change and search for novelty.[7] The implied superficial and ephemeral quality is, in part, why this has been neglected as a subject worthy of documentation or critical analysis. Furthermore, because of its links to western capitalist societies, fashion has also been associated with individualism, class distinction, and, is perceived as a marker of the progression of civilization, thus resulting in the exclusion of non-western societies from the wider discourse at an early stage in the development of fashion histories.[8] For the consumer, fashion is a medium of identification, allowing the wearer to be identified as part of a group or sharing a lifestyle, as well as a differentiating medium, allowing the constant re-definition of an individual's social status in relation to other groups in society.[9] Inspired by recent studies of fashion and national identity across the globe such as Alison Goodrum's, *The National Fabric: Fashion, Britishness, Globalization*, Juanjuan Wu's, *Chinese Fashion: From Mao to Now,* and Suzanne Gott and Kristyne Loughran's, *Contemporary African Fashion,* this chapter offers a survey of the work of key Indian designers practising over the last fifteen years: It will explore their role in the construction of identity and of fashion as a signifier of a particular time and space.[10]

The formation of the National Institute of Fashion Technology in Delhi in 1986 was the first step in fashion becoming a recognized industry and profession. In the post-liberalization period the institutional framework for the functioning of the industry developed through the Fashion

Design Council of India; set up in 1998 they initiated the Lakmé Fashion Week, the first ever in India, which took place in 2000 in Delhi. In 2005 Lakmé shifted to Mumbai and Wills Fashion Week was established in Delhi. With the subsequent addition of a number of other fashion weeks there is now a continuous circle of annual fashion events. A boost to the indigenous fashion media came in the 1990s with the arrival of international magazines *Elle* and *Cosmopolitan*; such competition pushing *Eve's Weekly* and *Femina* into becoming more fashion focused. These were joined in 1996 by *Verve*, which offered international production values and a more metropolitan outlook. They claimed to have 'pioneered a revolution in the depiction of contemporary Indian fashion, through stylized shoots that are international in approach and individual in execution'.[11] The entry of *Vogue* into India in 2007 was hailed as a validation of the Indian fashion system. Although predominantly selling international luxury labels to the rising middle-classes, the interspersing of Indian stories serves to nourish the local fashion industry. Websites and blogs add to the fashion media, their immediacy enabling them to be the first to communicate the nature of change in this field. *High Heel Confidential*, for example, is quick to relay regular fashion week highlights.[12] Offering a different perspective is *Wearabout*, a street-fashion blog run by the photographer Manou.[13] His discerning eye locates the fashionable in the ordinary and it helps to personalize an industry that promotes exclusivity.

Alongside education, institutional support and media promotion, retail spaces are fundamental to fashion. Boutiques and luxury shopping malls are two ends of the retailing spectrum currently making an impact in India. Shopping malls such as DLF Emporio in Delhi are extensive and exclusive allowing Indian and international brands to share the same building but offering the much feared homogenized global experience. Boutiques located in the metropolitan centres offer a more personal fashion experience and are situated in areas that foster a localized milieu for the nurturing, mediation and consumption of fashion. In Delhi these locations include Lodhi Colony or Santushti complex, with outlets by designers such as Rajesh Pratap Singh and Manish Arora. Hauz Khas sells a mixture of more experimental and traditional fashions. In Mumbai fashion environments are to be found at the Courtyard at Colaba and the South Mumbai area; with the Cinnamon Store and Rain Tree offering the same in Bengaluru. The design of retail interiors is part of the experience: Rajesh Pratap Singh's shops are ultra-simple white-box

Facing page:
Priyanka Bose. Model/Actress at Dadar Flower Market, Mumbai.
Photograph by Manou, 2011, courtesy wearabout/Manou.

37

spaces, but rather than offering bland universalism their inclusion of quirky innovative elements such as lighting and tables from medical equipment suppliers convey elegance and creativity. In his Vasant Kunj store, which opened in 2008, Lotus, a Delhi-based firm headed by Ambrish Arora, created decorative jali-screens using hundreds of open scissors sourced from the local markets, cleverly referencing notions of tailoring, the hand-made, and craftsmanship. Fashion retailing was established in Mumbai in 1987 when Tarun and Sal Tahiliani opened the multi-designer store Ensemble. In the recent story of Indian fashion, one of the most impactful boutiques is Bombay Electric. Established in 2006, it represents cosmopolitanism within the fashion industry; a quality personified in its owner, Priya Kishore, who, having grown-up in the UK, feels equally at home in London, Mumbai and elsewhere.[14] The shop, based in a heritage building, has a simple white interior in which Kishore stocks individually selected pieces that convey a global-local synthesis. Numerous press articles have projected the spirit of Bombay Electric as 'cutting edge' and a symbol of 'new Indian cool'.[15] All of these fashion retail spaces have been fundamental in constructing a cosmopolitan environment for the shaping of an Indian cosmopolitan identity.

It is in this setting that fashion designers operate, they feed from it and they contribute to it. The responsiveness of Indian designers to an increasingly globalized world is reflective of their own cosmopolitan positions. Located within the cities of Mumbai, Delhi, Kolkata, and Bengaluru, they are connected to the rest of India and beyond through their studies, training, travels, through the people they interact with, through the flow of ideas, images, concepts and knowledge they have access to via the internet, international publications, satellite television and other forms of global communication.

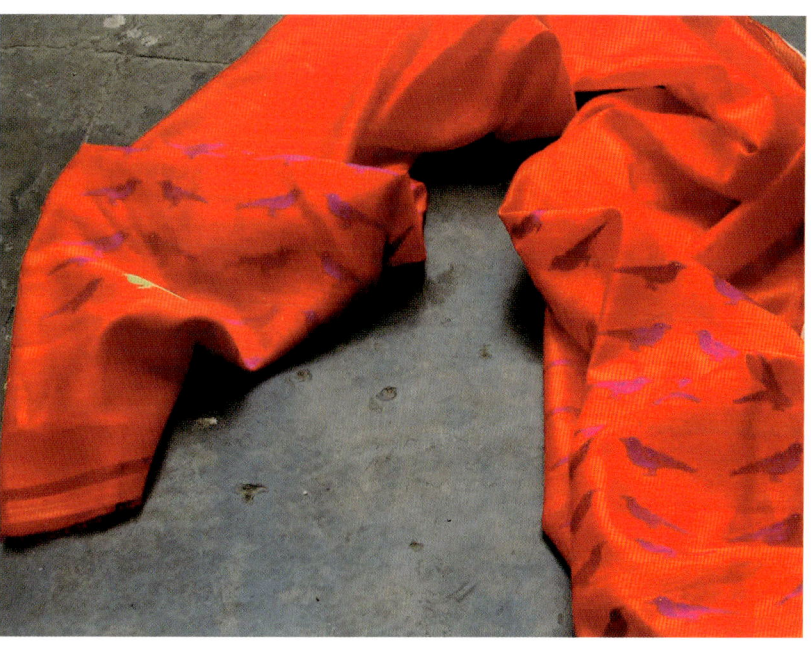

NATIONAL FASHION CLASSICS

Facing page:
White sari with green and
gold border.
Designed by Sanjay Garg,
Raw Mango.
Silk and cotton, hand-woven
in Chanderi, Madhya Pradesh,
2010.
Photo courtesy Sanjay Garg,
Raw Mango.

Above:
Orange sari with crow motif.
Designed by Sanjay Garg,
Raw Mango.
Silk and cotton, hand-woven
in Chanderi, Madhya Pradesh,
2010.
Photo courtesy Sanjay Garg,
Raw Mango.

'**The sari** with its seamless folded rigour, and the kurta, with its classic agelessness, are fashion classics that do exactly what great design should do: Empower you to move efficiently and glamorously through the day.' This quote by Sally Singer of American *Vogue*, in the first edition of *Vogue* India, though typical of glossy magazines in its generalization, sums up the global recognition of two of India's most important national fashion stories.[16] The sari is perceived to be the most iconic, traditional and unchanging item of clothing in India. A simple unstitched length of fabric that when draped becomes a beautiful and elegant symbol of national identity, with the flexibility to reflect regional diversity and social individuality. It is a garment of protection and seduction, a symbol of chaste purity as it wraps and covers the Hindu goddess, or a symbol of the seductress as it adorns and reveals the film actress.[17] However, contrary to popular belief in its ancient 'time-less' lineage, the sari as recognized today with its petticoat and tight-fitting blouse, known as the *nivi* style, is located to the early 20th century, and pan-Indian awareness of it is attributed to the Indian cinema.[18] It is also not, as is perceived in the West, an effortless garment to wear: it often requires pins to keep the pleating and folding in place. Over time, the sari has adapted to region, climate, and practical needs. Thus, far

41

Pink sari with lotus motif.
Designed by Sanjay Garg,
Raw Mango.
Silk and cotton, hand-woven
in Chanderi, Madhya Pradesh,
2010.
Photo courtesy Sanjay Garg,
Raw Mango.

from being frozen in time, it is a signifier of change, reacting to different environments and different contexts.

Within the present urban context, professional women navigate global office spaces and cosmopolitan city environments, as well as sites of traditional interactions such as festivals, family gatherings and life-cycle rituals. Their clothing enables them to shift from one identity to another through these incongruent spaces. Designers are re-interpreting the sari in a multitude of ways, adapting them to these more fluid contemporary lifestyles. In doing so, the sari has become at once an 'elevated' form of dress, conferring on the wearer a value of authenticity and tradition, as well as a highly adaptable contemporary garment.[19]

Sanjay Garg and his company Raw Mango seek to create a fashionable image ideal for the 'intelligent, independent and non-materialistic woman looking for an alternative form of Indian expression'.[20] Fundamental to his contemporising of the sari is a desire to re-popularize it, to make it appeal to a younger generation. His design interventions focus on simplifying traditional motifs and experimenting with handloom weaving to make lighter and more wearable saris. From the careful study of antique textiles and paintings, Garg isolates motifs such as the mango tree, the lotus, the cow, and the *phulkari*-flower and makes a feature of them, usually only on the *pallou*, with the main body of the sari kept plain. His signature design is that of the Indian crow, woven 108 times in rows across the *pallou*, with one bird woven in a contrasting colour. The saris are impactful because of the sharp and often bright colour combinations that require no further decoration. This counteracts the trends for over-embellished Bollywood kitsch or certain types of modern handloom fabrics which can be thick and relatively difficult to drape. The majority of his saris are woven with the silk weft and cotton warp and are left un-starched to make the fabric softer and more pliable, enabling it to be worn as a figure-hugging garment that appeals to the modern woman.

Launched in 2009, Raw Mango has made a significant impact in the sari industry. Central to the company's success is the marketing of the product where equal weight is given to selling the modernity of the product as to the tradition of village-based craftsmanship that underpins it. 'Raw Mango is not just about design, it is about a larger programme that has managed to up-lift an entire community by creating a new value

Jiyo! Abstract sari from the
Pochampally Ikat Collection.
Designed by Hitesh Rawat &
Avanish Kumar for *Jiyo!*
Silk, ikat, hand-woven by
Jella Sudharkar in Guttapal,
Pochampally, Andhra Pradesh,
2011-12.
Photo courtesy V&A Museum,
London.

Facing page:
Jiyo! Pebble-Stream sari.
Designed by Swati Kalsi
for *Jiyo!*
Silk, hand-embroidered by
Guriya Kumari, Rani Kumari,
Anisa Kumari, and Khushboo
Kumari in Bihar, 2011-12.
Photo courtesy V&A Museum,
London.

for an existing or ignored product'.[21] They work with a group of weavers in Chanderi, a long established weaving centre in Madhya Pradesh, central India, used to producing traditional Chanderi saris. Raw Mango's engagement with them has resulted in an expansion from utilizing four looms to over one hundred and the employment of some three hundred craftsmen. To ensure the smooth running of the process, Garg visits the unit about three times a month and interacts with the managers and the weavers. Gaining a proper appreciation of their skills and experiences helps to achieve the finest results whilst remain true to the textiles and technique. Here, design intervention, through a developed understanding, has created new value in an old product.[22] A sense of this new value is projected through the promotional images which offer a relaxed, confident modern representation of the Indian woman. They use self-assured women in non-glamorous locations, with the styling of the sari done in a nonchalant manner, wearing non-revealing blouses and an elegantly messy *pallou* roughly thrown over the shoulder. The photographs capture the infusion of the ordinary with something a little bit special. Alongside the Chanderi range, Sanjay Garg has developed sari collections that are inspired by Banarasi silks as well as the *mashru* weaving technique.

For *Jiyo!*, 'a swadeshi brand for the 21st century', the sari is a national symbol of identity and a product which has the capability to revive small village economies. *Jiyo!* was established in 2007 as a creative, economic and social development initiative, building on the long tradition of non-government organizations developing a more ethical and less exploitative way of working with India's large body of crafts people. Aligning itself to the Swadeshi movement of 1905 which boycotted foreign goods in favour of Indian products which culminated in the struggle for independence, *Jiyo*'s Gandhian vision to compete against the current influx of luxury western brands into India has resulted in the production of some high-end, heritage-linked saris that contribute towards a sustainable livelihood. Their impact lies not in changing attitudes towards popularizing the sari, but in the development of an integrated design process.[23]

Jiyo's design response to their perceived fear of the homogenizing and economically destructive forces of globalization is to deactivate them through dynamic hand-crafted local processes. The rhythmic simplicity of *sujini* embroidery, a basic running stitch used by the women of Bihar to patch together old fabric and garments into quilts, is transformed into

46

a luxury garment. Designer Swati Kalsi transplants this technique onto tussar silk, devising designs that are an exploration of organic forms and patterns inspired by nature. Playing with variations in the length and spacing of stitches enables her to create dense and loose coverage from which evolve areas of mass and void. The designs are flexible enough to enable the untrained artisans to develop their own creativity and confidence, making this a collaborative project rather than one imposed by the trained designer.[24] One of the key markers of success for the project will be when the designer is able to walk away in the knowledge that future production will remain at the high quality established during the training.[25] *Jiyo*'s ikat range, designed by Hitesh Rawat and Avanish Kumar, juxtaposes blocks of colour of varying sizes with apparent randomness. The bold abstraction of the ikats, along with the intricate yet deceptively random quality of the *sujini*, conveys a very successful amalgamation of a contemporary aesthetic with a traditional technique.

An edgier look for the young urban female has been created by Abraham and Thakore. This is a direct result of the changing economic climate in India which saw them expand in 2007 from being a long established export-driven design company to a more fashion focussed one aimed at the burgeoning Indian market. Each subsequent collection has included a range of saris within their repertoire of simple silhouettes. Their saris are shorter in length, made to a four-yard rather than the usual six-yard length, which makes them less bulky to wear. A trademark is the use of dramatic black and white handloom fabrics juxtaposed with a block colour, such as shocking yellow or bright red. These are often teamed with short padded jackets or shirts and belts, which gives them an unconventional, quirky twist. Many of their handloom fabrics are produced by weaving communities in West Bengal and Andhra Pradesh. For the Autumn/Winter 2011/12 Collection they produced a spectacular silk fabric which imitated the traditional British tessellated houndstooth pattern using the complex process of double-ikat weaving. This was made possible because of their long-term association with the weaving community in Andhra Pradesh. The transference of a design associated with classic western menswear into a handwoven silk sari, and teamed with a long-sleeved shirt makes it into a stylish, clever, and bold blend of cross-cultural influences. The same collection included a range of saris in chiffons with classic menswear prints.[26] Subsequent collections have continued to celebrate handloom weaving, with designs focussing on bold geometric shapes.

Facing page:
Rickshaw sari.
Designed by Abraham
and Thakore.
Silk, jamdani inlay, hand-woven
in the co-operative of Nutan
Fulia Tantubay Samabay
Samity Ltd., West Bengal.
Autumn/Winter 2010-11
Collection.
Photo courtesy Abraham
and Thakore.

Houndstooth sari.
Designed by Abraham
and Thakore.
Silk, double ikat, hand-woven
in workshops of master
weaver, Goverdhan of Murli
Saree Emporium, Hyderabad,
Andhra Pradesh.
Autumn/Winter 2011-12
Collection.
Photo courtesy Abraham
and Thakore.

49

Handprint detail from sari.
Designed by Masaba Gupta.
Silk, block printed, 2011.
Photo courtesy V&A Museum,
London.

Facing page:
Sari from the Caravan
Collection.
Designed by Nacihket Barve.
Autumn/Winter 2012.
Photo courtesy Nachiket Barve.

Alternative methods of contemporizing the sari can be seen in the work of Masaba Gupta, Nida Mahmood, and Nachiket Barve. They construct six-yard lengths from smaller pieces of fabric that are sewn together, mixing a variety of textures and textiles. Both designers have very different aesthetics: Masaba's dramatic saris consist of blocks of simple colour against blocks of bold pattern; she incorporates sections of synthetic netting and a contrasting silk border that unites the whole. When worn the front pleating is often of a different material than the *pallou*. Her trademark fabric, drawn from her childhood memories of playing with hand prints, is a repeat block-print of a human hand. This was notably used to great effect in her first collection when worn as a petticoat underneath a transparent net sari which was adorned with a little pocket on the side – adding a quirky touch to the ensemble. Nida Mahmood's saris consist mainly of vertical strips of fabrics which are often embroidered and sequinned, taking their influence from vintage Gujarati sari borders. With their contrasting bright colours, they convey her popular culture aesthetic but also have a delicacy in their detailing. Mahmood styles her saris with jeans, and although this is a gimmick used in fashion shows, they project a sense of the contemporary urban

Facing page:
Suicide Print sari with Random
Suicide waistcoat and
Shoetread underskirt.
Suicide and Random Suicide
Print designed by Kallol Datta
and Indranil Ram Kamath.
Shoetread Print designed by
Kallol Datta.
Silk screen print.
Autumn/Winter 2011.
Photo courtesy
Kallol Datta 1955.

Right:
Sari from the Bohemian
Tamasha Collection.
Designed by Nida Mahmood.
Spring/Summer 2012.
Photo courtesy Nida Mahmood.

environment in which she places herself and her customers.[27] Nachiket Barve uses a wealth of global influences in his saris: the 'Caravan' range, showcased in 2012, draws on the connectivity of the ancient trade routes and borrows motifs from Islamic woodwork, tiling, and carpets. He combines a range of techniques in the different sections of the sari, including tie-dye, *mashru* weaving, elaborate embroidery, and beadwork.

Offering a very different perspective by questioning the stereotypical notions of beauty and glamour is the work of Kallol Datta. He develops bold, humorous, often controversial prints which are silk-screened onto the sari fabric. His saris are teamed with loose-fitting de-constructed blouses that are the very opposite of the usual small, well-fitted, midriff-exposing tops. Occasionally they cover the entire top half of the sari, thus obscuring much of the drape that defines it. These adaptations subvert the conventions of sari-wearing, acknowledging alternative body types and sub-cultural identities. The re-design and re-contextualization of the sari into these multiple contemporary manifestations demonstrate the responsiveness of designers to a changing environment. The capability of the sari to survive constant recreation is further evidenced in the structured sari-gowns of Gaurav Gupta, which amalgamate the Indian drape with the western evening gown. The wider acceptance of these adaptations to what has been perceived as a traditional non-changing symbol of national identity is a more fundamental responsiveness to globalization as it encompasses a strengthening of confidence in images of the self, in women's changing position within the metropolitan cities, and reflects the cosmopolitan nature of the times.

The adaptability of the sari is more than matched by the infinite possibilities offered by the conflation of the shalwar kameez, kurta churidar, and other tunic/trouser ensembles. The shalwar kameez, consisting of baggy loose trousers gathered at the ankles and worn underneath a long tunic, with a dupatta (long scarf) across the shoulders, is associated with Islamic dress and mainly seen in Punjab and north India. Other stylistic variations as represented in the kurta (male and female long shirt), kurti (female short shirt) and churidar (narrow male or female trousers), and *angarakha* (male long shirt), are regionally linked to Rajasthan. Since the 1980s the shalwar kameez has been increasingly worn as a uniform by school girls and it proliferates in office spaces; while the kurta over jeans has become the common dress of young women attending college. The result has been a gradual erosion of earlier

Facing page:
Kurta Pyjama.
Designed by Abraham and Thakore.
Cotton & linen blend.
Spring/Summer 2011.
Photo courtesy Abraham and Thakore.

55

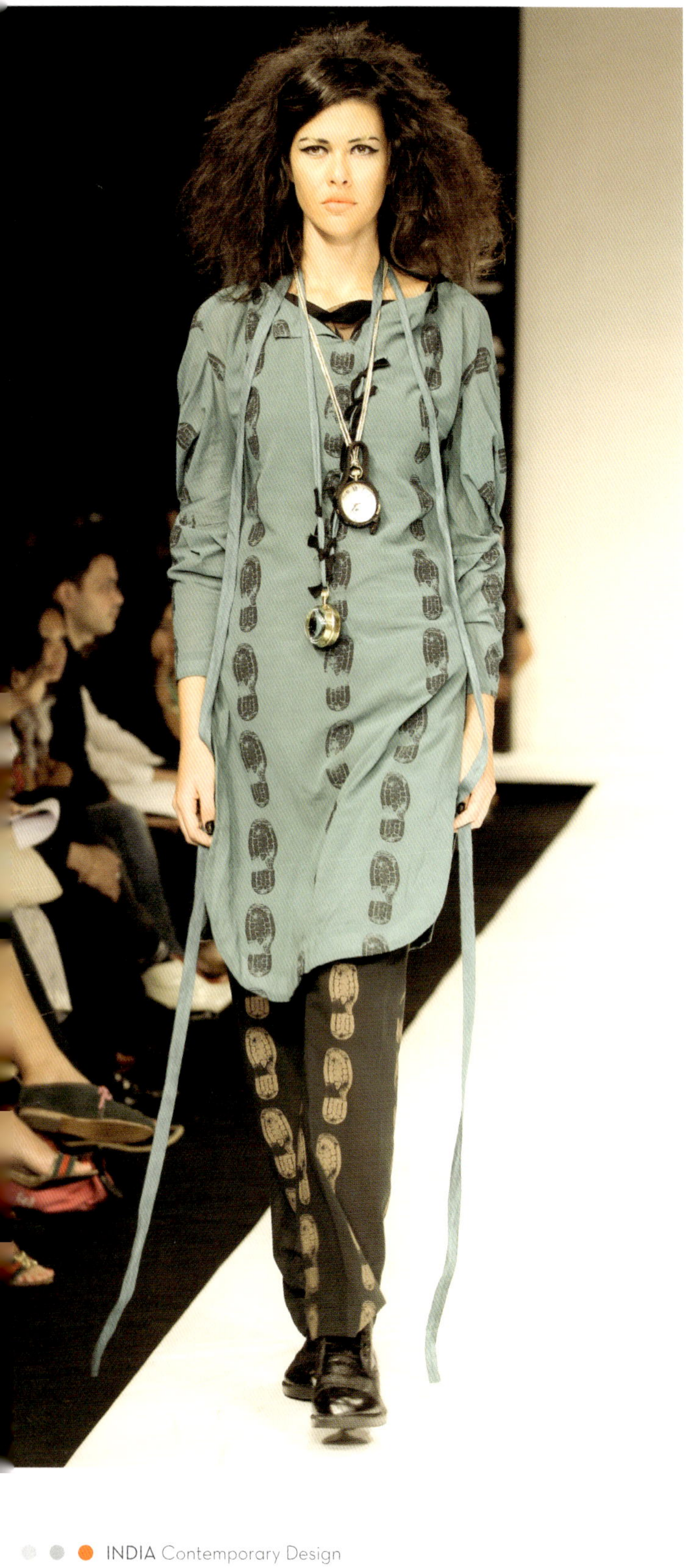

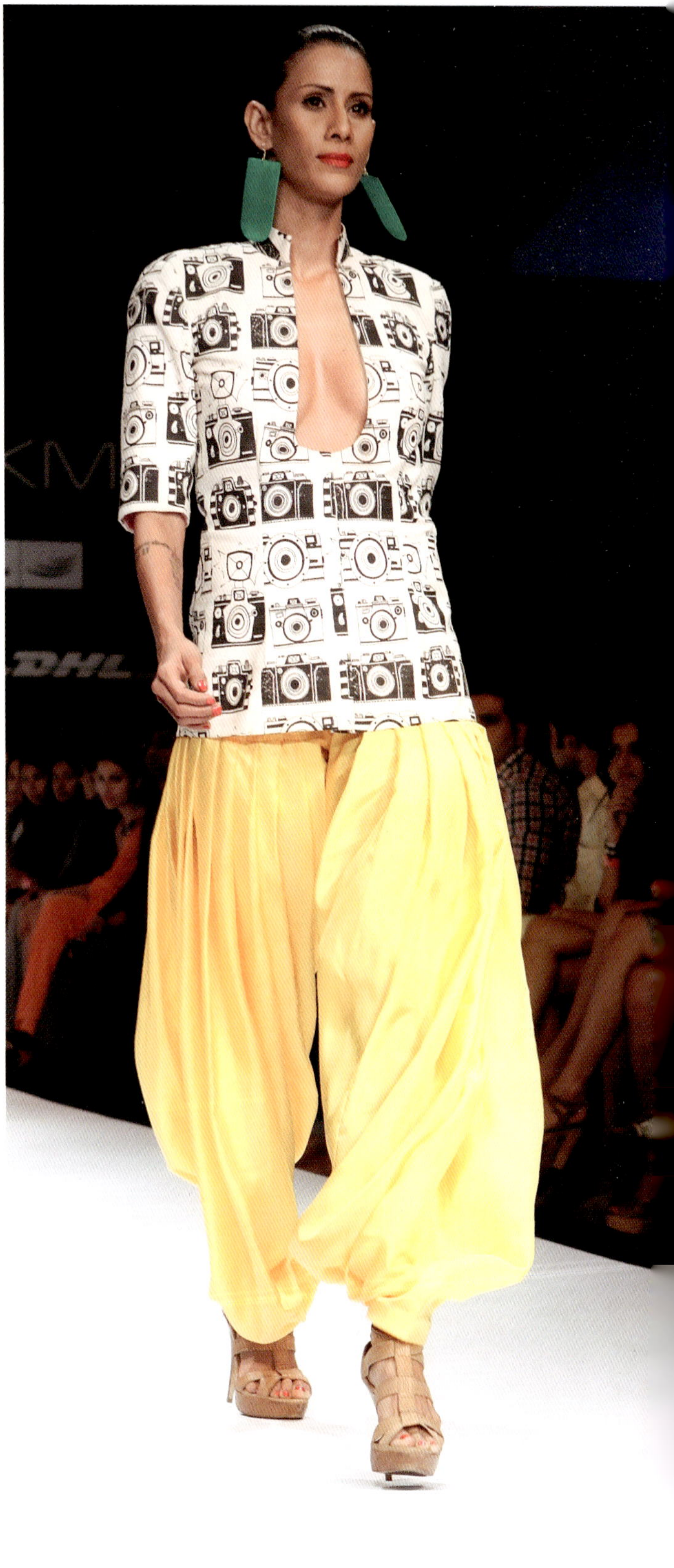

Facing page:
Left: Shoetread 3D fold tunic
with shoetread cargo trousers.
Designed by Kallol Datta.
Silk screen print.
Autumn/Winter 2011.
Photo courtesy
Kallol Datta 1955.

Right: Patiala-style shalwar.
Designed by
Masaba Gupta, 2012.
Photo courtesy Getty Images.

associations and the spread of versions of this form of dress across India and across generations. Its ubiquity makes it the single most important and noticeable factor of change in fashion over the last two decades. Functionality is at the heart of this shift: while the sari is adaptable, the shalwar kameez/ kurta churidar are perceived as being more practical within an urban environment and therefore more modern, suggesting an alternative national dress.[28]

The qualities of functionality and adaptability are fully utilized by designers where experimentation and deconstruction of the tunic, trouser and scarf ensemble allow them to project modernity and modesty. The kurti, for example, is celebrated because it 'takes one simple idea – an essentially Indian idea – and adapts it for a global audience *without* losing the inherent Indian touch'.[29] Its permeation into the wider world is recognized where 'versions of tunics over pants are pretty standard in international fashion'.[30] An example of this can be seen in a *Vogue* magazine picture story where for the 2007 season 'churi pants with bangle-like folds at the ankle made appearances on the catwalks from Gucci to Chanel'.[31] For many designers this set of clothing is their most profitable and tends to dominate their ready-to-wear ranges. Here too, designers are able to project a sense of identity. The Indian-ness of the ensemble has been expressed very dynamically through the work of Masaba Gupta; her 'patiala'-style shalwars, defined by their pleating and overlapping, tulip-edged shape, have become one of her bestsellers. Sold individually in a series of colours and patterns to be paired with a variety of tops, they demonstrate the versatility of the garment. A greater number of designers, however, have expressed their international outlook through the ensemble: Abraham and Thakore have excelled in this field, mixing different trouser widths with lengths of kurta in their trademark hand-woven fabrics to create very contemporary urban outfits. Aneeth Arora's collections deconstruct further and add impact through multiple layering of texture and pattern. Kallol Dutta's bold prints and non-conventional cuts create dramatic silhouettes. These latter examples demonstrate that versatility and infinite variation promote the fusion of the Indian with the international in terms of identity and aesthetic.

CRAFTING FASHION

For generations of designers the location of a unique identity, of tradition and of authenticity is to be found in *karigari* or craftsmanship as embodied in India's handloom weavers, embroiderers and the wealth of skilled, often village-based communities. The first generation of designers that included Ritu Kumar, Rohit Bal, Tarun Tahiliani, and Asha Sarabhai built their reputations on the re-interpretation of India's rich heritage. They emerged in the 1980s into an environment informed by revivalist policies and craft-promotion led by influential figures such as Kamladevi Chattopadhyaya and Pupul Jayakar. Their work with craft-communities was shaped by the debates of the time and they created classic Indian chic, repositioning dying craft skills into sought-after luxury high-end fashions.[32] They generated a belief in the strength of Indian resources and skills. Subsequent generations have re-contextualized it within their social, economic, and political time frames.

In an article entitled 'Indian designers make their mark with craft', the international fashion critic Suzy Menkes in the *New York Times*, 29 March 2009, highlights one of the key differentiating mechanisms of India's creative communities. Today's designers still believe that *karigari* is India's great strength as it continues to symbolize embedded knowledge, creativity, skill, material, technique, and diversity, and they see its potential as a unique force capable of change and innovation. A series of interviews recorded in 2007 revealed that, for many designers, the application of an imaginative and intelligent approach can lead to a metamorphosis from which emerge new ways of looking at tradition.[33] In their engagement with, and exploration of, materials, method, embellishment and structure, designers demonstrate the multiple ways of contemporizing tradition.

Rajesh Pratap Singh offers some of the most striking and innovative explorations of India's textile heritage. His fashions are evidence of his training in Italy as well as his inherent Indian-ness. Of particular interest are his sharp western-cut suits, which are layered with print and pattern that is Indian but has a strong western resonance. The

Facing page:
Men's *Gamcha* jacket.
Designed by Rajesh Pratap Singh
Silk, cotton & linen blend.
Spring/Summer 2009.
Photo courtesy Rajesh Pratap Singh.

59

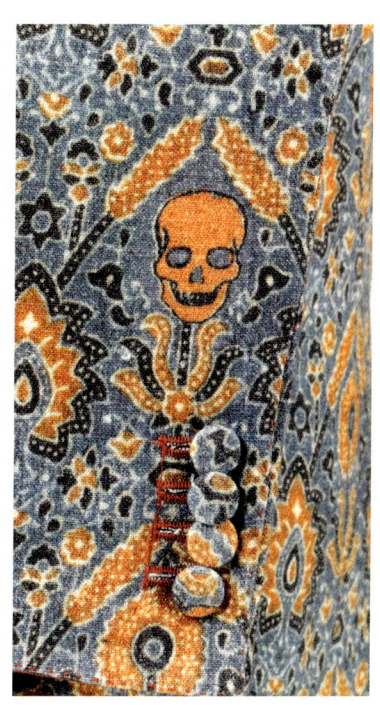

dialogue within these pieces speaks of the exchange of ideas and imagery as well as skill and technique. They are illustrative of the layering of meaning that occurs in designs that are global and local in outlook. The *Gamcha* suit, for example, is made from silk and cotton fabric that has been handwoven in his workshops. It takes inspiration from the common *gamcha* cloth, a coarse cotton towel, checked with red and white or other colour combinations and used by working men for multiple purposes including wiping sweat from the body. Tradition is located not only in the weaving technique; it is also in the use of the *gamcha* in daily routine. In taking a common fabric, transforming it through its production in silk and elevating it to high fashion through its western cut, the designer has invested an Indian and western identity into the suit.

A more complex construction of identity is to be found in the '*Ajrakh*' jacket. To a western eye, the jacket has a quirky elegance defined by the tailoring and the detailing on the collar and the pockets. To the Indian eye, the *ajrakh* print gives an immediate link to heritage. The indigo blue background with red patterning is characteristic of the block printing technique specific to western India and Pakistan.[34] From a distance the patterning appears to be a repetitive floral design typical of *ajrakh* fabrics; however, subtly integrated into the floral repeats are depictions of the human skull. This skull imagery is derived from European fashion and art: once part of rock music sub-culture, incorporated into high-fashion through the designer Alexander McQueen and art through Damien Hurst, it has been diffused into everyday accessories and become ubiquitous, losing its connection to death. In India the skull is found in images of Hindu gods Shiva and Kali and keeps its deathly associations. The process of *ajrakh* is long and time consuming taking up to thirty steps to complete. A key part of this is the making of the wooden blocks that transfer the pattern onto the fabric, several of which are needed for each design and colour. Carving the blocks requires skill and is executed by a different group of people than the dyers. In this instance the designer searched for a block-maker who was willing to carve the skull image: many of the Muslim block-makers would not facilitate this because of their prohibition against creating representational figures as well as the associations to death. Therefore, to realize his imagined article, Rajesh transferred to digital printing, a technical process that has

enabled the cross fertilization of design and culture.[35] Through the fusion of tradition and technology, the jacket becomes a symbol of the times representing both global and temporal flows.

Engagement and experimentation with Indian textile and clothing traditions are the basis of one of the most successful of the younger generation of designers, Aneeth Arora.[36] Through her fashion label *Péro* she experiments with tie-dye, ikat, block printing, jamdani weaving, fine muslins and more. Arora has gained much critical success since her first collection was showcased in 2008. She takes her inspiration from the craftsmen, not only as a body of highly skilled individuals, but also through their own clothing in which she sees a natural and graceful purity. 'Most garments are inspired by local dressing styles that one comes across in the remotest of areas – they are the real trend setters of the time – for theirs is an effortless style'.[37] Her trademark is the light, loosely constructed structures of her clothing executed in subtle, muted shades with delicate print, patterns, and textures. Deriving inspiration from crafts and traditional textile production is only part of the design story; engagement with craft communities to implement the designs and realize the garments is equally important. Arora has spent time in villages seeing samples and developing the right process for her fabrics. Designers often face multiple hurdles with village-based production: factors such as seasonal rains, cultural functions, weddings, and religious festivals can stop production for periods of time, which affects the supply chain, and in turn affects any contractual relationships the designer may have established with retail outlets. The need to be present for a significant period of time within the village to ensure the quality of the product can be demanding and restrictive to the expansion of the business.

As a consequence, most designers choose to work directly with mastercraftsmen. This is a difficult term to define as their skills and responsibilities change across regions and across media. It refers to a person in a position of power over a set of craftsmen; they will be the middleman who coordinate the supply of work, they negotiate pricing, and are responsible for delivery of finished work. In some cases the mastercraftsman is also a practitioner who excels at his skill; in other instances he is more of a businessman with no experience of the craft itself. Designers can communicate

Facing page:
Dress layered over slip.
Designed by Aneeth Arora
for Péro.
Dress: hand-woven jamdani
fabric, West Bengal.
Slip: reverse bandhani,
Kutch, Gujarat.
Spring/Summer 2010.
Photo courtesy Aneeth Arora.

Above:
Sample booklet and postcards
for Péro.
Spring/Summer 2010.
Photo courtesy
V&A Museum, London.

their needs to the mastercraftsman and he, with his knowledge of the village weavers will be able to realize the order. The mastercraftsmen system and can be in the form of co-operatives or be more exploitative; in either case it is problematic.[38] Although Arora uses the services of mastercraftsmen, illustrative of the personal relationship with craft communities is her work with a group of weavers in West Bengal who produce *jamdani* fabrics – extremely fine muslin with delicate motifs. When she first started using the material she found that the complicated process took one weaver one week to produce three metres of fabric. There are now thirty weavers producing for her and she feels some responsibility in keeping them employed. They enjoy working with this technique and she has instilled pride in their work through creating a market for their skills. Thus, each one of her collections will include some *jamdani* fabric.[39]

Péro's design philosophy is centred on 'utilizing indigenous skills and knowledge of ancient textiles'.[40] For her, 'The Indian-ness of *Péro* rests in the textile process, where materials pass through the hands of one craftsman to another, carrying forward the Indian tradition of the handmade and creating pieces that are at once unique'.[41] Here, a romantic and idealized image of village tradition is used as a mark of authenticity, uniqueness, and identity. It relies on the notion of 'timeless India' as constructed during the nationalist movement and through which villagers become the keepers of a continuous, isolated, and static tradition located in antiquity.[42]

In the promotion of her fashions, she focuses on the textile traditions rather than the glamour of new and daring silhouettes. To convey the primacy of the fabrics and the concept of the hand-crafted, she distributes samples during her fashion shows in novel ways. This has included beautiful hand-made books filled with fabric swatches and a text that acknowledged their regional variety, as well as toy rickshaws filled with miniature rolls of textiles.[43] The promotion of her clothing is centred on a pairing of Indian-ness and universality, their consumption targeted at both local and global markets: 'The resulting garment evokes some sense of the culture from which it originates. This culture communicates internationally in such a way that the wearer looks equally at ease in Paris and London, as she does here in India'.[44] It is the concept of excellent and subtle craftsmanship, the

Facing page:
Dress and shirt.
Designed by Aneeth Arora
for Péro.
Dress: hand-woven jamdani
fabric, West Bengal.
Shirt: khadi checks.
Spring/Summer 2010.
Photo courtesy Aneeth Arora.

64

Dress with lotus-print motif.
Designed by Rahul Mishra.
Silk, hand-woven in Chanderi,
Madhya Pradesh.
Spring/Summer 2011.
Photo courtesy Rahul Mishra.

Facing page:
Waistcoat and skirt ensemble.
Designed by Shenali Sema.
Khadi, hand-stiched, 2010.
Photo courtesy Devika
Dwarkadas and Shenali Sema.

romance and luxury of the handmade, that brings global appeal to fashion that is so locally situated.

The romance of the handmade is epitomized in khadi. This hand-spun, hand-woven fabric, symbolic of the nationalist movement, resonates with meaning, and its appeal is such that many designers (e.g. Rahul Mishra, Paromita Banerjee) incorporate khadi pieces into their collections. Rajesh Pratap Singh has experimented with it for many years. In his workshops he has developed an extremely high-count khadi which is used to produce beautifully fine, almost diaphanous garments.[45] However, khadi is deeply problematic: its handspun and handwoven quality make it a relatively expensive fabric; the sheer beauty and simplicity of the cloth, without the embellishment of sequins or embroidery, appeals to a niche group of connoisseurs, thereby counteracting the egalitarian principles for which it was originally produced.[46]

Exploring through the lens of environmental sustainability, Shenali Sema and Priyanka Patel fashioned a set of garments which took the concepts of no-waste and the handmade to their furthest points. They choose to work with un-dyed khadi because of its minimal impact on the environment and to use lengths specifically woven for dhotis. The dhoti is a garment that is finished on the loom; once woven to a length of four metres, it requires no further intervention before it can be used for draping around the lower half of the male body. The design challenge was in creating other garments from it without leaving waste. Thus, each one-piece or two-piece outfit is made from one dhoti. Their carefully planned cutting and construction resulted in only small scraps, which were then used in subtle embellishment. The selvedge, which is normally discarded when making garments, is made into a feature, and occasionally a simple line of embroidery is used to give visual interest. Much of their inspiration for the fine detailing on the edges and the hemming came from antique muslin garments. Adding a further layer of complexity to their work, they personally hand-stitched all of the garments, thus enabling them to appreciate the slow and meditative nature of the hand-making process. Although this was a diploma project for the NID, it encompasses the fundamental issues of working with khadi, playing on its romantic associations and highlighting the problematic dichotomy of the non-affordability of the hand-made versus the mass-produced.[47]

Handloom fabrics and craft traditions are used by many other designers, all of whom convey Indian-ness through their work. They include Rahul Mishra, whose first collection, entitled 'Let craft lead the way', explored western silhouettes in Maheshwari fabrics; and his subsequent collections have focused on different group of artisans from different regions. An alternative craft-based approach is employed by Nachiket Barve in his use of more complex and detailed embellishments produced from a variety of textile techniques and by Small Shop in their use of resist-dyed prints on unusual silhouettes combined with a distinct colour palate. However, it is in the work of Sabyasachi Mukherjee that we see the most overt expression of an Indian identity.

Sabyasachi's design philosophy is concentrated into the slogan 'the personalized imperfection of the human hand', that unique mark made by a crafts person that distinguishes what he creates from the mass produced.[48] One of India's most successful and important designers he has, over the last ten years, built his reputation on the use of handloom and other traditional techniques. His early success on the international scene, in Milan and New York, was recognition of his highly original combination of Indian hand-crafted techniques and contemporary western cuts. Disillusionment with the international fashion industry in 2009, and aware of the shift in economic power in favour of India, he turned his attention exclusively to the domestic market, stating that 'As India's economy booms and pride in our nation surges, Indian fashion is looking inwards. Instead of mimicking western traditions, we must look into our own past and grapple with our identity'.[49] His unique design signature is the layering and clever juxtaposition of multiple textiles and textures, deep hues, vintage appearance, beautifully crafted embroidery, and an overall luxurious glamour. These designs are an unashamed celebration of Indian textiles. Sabyasachi's incomparable skill is in envisioning, reinventing and utilizing the adaptability of the traditional craft aesthetic.

Sabyasachi has built his reputation on creating heirloom pieces, saris and classic Indian silhouettes for the luxury market; but he has developed his business success on the wedding trousseau. Characterized by abundant and intricate gold and silver work, sequins, and multiple rich, dense, embroidery techniques, his

designs are much sought after. Weddings are both a key factor in the development of fashion in India and in the preservation of Indian embroidery techniques. Today, most designers make their greatest profit through wedding outfits; these are specially commissioned one-off pieces, often termed 'Indian couture' because of their exclusivity, personalization, use of expensive fabrics and extensive hand-crafted embellishment. The visual realization of a wedding trousseau is inspired by a variety of sources which include surviving examples, most of which date from the early 20th century, to historical costume found in museums and publications, as well as photographs and paintings. The extreme embellishment seen on many of Sabyasachi's clothes is constructed from such historical referencing; it is an amalgamation and evolution of these traditions. The commissioning of such elaborate outfits and the copious amount of money spent on such occasions is a sign of the times and is a reflection of the aspirations of the rising middle class.[50] 'The wedding, as a signifier of social status, gets more and more powerful as the Indian economy creates more and more consumers for luxury'.[51] The desire to identify with an Indian elite is expressed through the emulation of lavish wedding ceremonies which reference the grandeur and 'traditions' of the maharajahs as well as those of modern-day royalty — Bollywood film stars. The fashionable, extravagant wedding, therefore, is a medium for class differentiation and identification.[52]

Called the 'clothes nationalist', Sabyasachi's collections are charged with a strongly patriotic mission: to promote pride in being Indian and to define an Indian identity through craft.[53] The *Chand Bibi* collection began his exploration of Indian silhouettes in a more focused way. The 2008 Bridal Sutra show urged his audience to preserve 'our tradition, our heritage, our legacy' by highlighting the ancient art of *patola*, double-ikat weaving. 'For over 750 years this exquisite fabric has adorned royalty across Asia. Today only four families remain that produce this queen of all silks. A precious Indian craft stands on the verge of extinction.... What can we do to preserve it?' The beauty of simple handspun fabrics, plain khadi saris and rough textures without embellishment was the focus in *Neela aur Bagardandi ki kahanni* (the blue or burgundy story), his 2009 collection. His most visually vocal patriotism came in 2010 with the show *Aparajito* 'the unvanquished', he proclaimed

'Indian textiles cannot be beaten, tradition cannot be beaten.'
The ramp show, prefaced with a screen that listed the featured
regional textiles, began with a playing of the national anthem with
scenes from the film *1947 Earth*. Even when his 2011 collection
was influenced by the international scene of the1960s and '70s
with silhouettes that were 'sports meets retro-rock', he was quick
to point out that the 'entire range uses Indian handicraft fabrics
like textured khadi, a little bit of zardozi, beaten and burnt crystals
and lace'. He sees his best means of helping craft revival is through
promotion and he is very vocal about his desire to help. 'Every year,
I try to work with a different craft sector and incorporate
their tradition into my collection. If you are an Indian designer
and don't respect indigenous craftsmen, then you are at best a
(western) wannabe'.[54]

Fashion and Popular Culture

A sense of identity is found not only in the craft traditions of India, it is also found in popular culture, on the streets, the everyday and the mundane.[55] Popular culture, that which has mass appeal, is defined by its proliferation and its familiarity. It includes everything from Bollywood films, music and television to Amar Chitra Katha comics, handpainted street signs and market stalls. Designers such as Manish Arora, Little Shilpa, and Nida Mahmood take their inspiration from popular culture and use it to create a distinctive aesthetic that engages with issues of identity on multiple levels.

Manish Arora: 'Design guru, maverick and king of kitsch'. This is the label given to him in the opening sequence of a television series made in 2008. The series title, *Travels of a Ladies Tailor*, immediately aligns Arora to a common profession from which the notion of the elite designer has arisen. The tailor, present across India in small booths in city streets and villages, is a fitting persona for a man who takes his inspiration from the streets and the common people. Part travelogue, part fashion documentary, the programme gives an insight into his process of consuming influences from across diverse Indian landscapes, and is evidence of the development of his distinct sensibility to the exuberant juxtaposition of colour, pattern, texture, and technique in those landscapes. As inspiration and expression, Manish Arora's fashion displays an unrivalled use of popular culture. He applies hyper-real colours: intensified hues drawn from calendar prints, folk images, textiles, and architecture. This is overlaid with motifs taken from the streets, from everyday life, from Indian popular culture and other popular cultures. Often there is the rhythmic repetition of motifs, shapes and cropped forms creating bursts and clusters of intense pattern. There is manipulation of scale as seen in the enlargement of faces from comic books complete with dialogue bubbles, or in mirror work embroidery that is over-sized and in the repetition of bindis into large spiralling circles of pattern. There is the application of multiple Indian techniques of embroidery, appliqué, and beading in a breathtaking level of detail. The brazen mixing of colours, intense pattern, and kitsch motif, executed with elaborate craftsmanship, has become his trademark.[56]

Facing page:
Pop-Art outfit.
Designed by Manish Arora.
Spring/Summer 2008.
Photo courtesy Manish Arora.

75

Arora's early collections (Paris 2008 in particular) made an overt use of a range of national symbols such as the ambassador taxi, lotus flowers, the Om sign, alongside regional symbols like the Orissan *Jagannath* and the Kerala dance mask. His use of identifiable regional embroidery techniques, such as the Gujarati mirror work, golden gota detailing and appliqué, all served to express Indian-ness. The application of these elements to western silhouettes appealed to an Indian market because it drew attention to the common and the everyday in a manner that had not been seen before. It offered a re-appropriation of Indian-ness, but one that was in opposition to the craft-based aesthetic of other designers. This expressly Indian aesthetic continues to feature in his fashion lines for Indian markets, and is incorporated into his other collaborative product ranges such as Nike shoes and Swatch watches. From this has arisen the distinct Arora brand, one of the strongest fashion brands in India and one that has a profile outside of India.

These clothes also express a global quality, not just through their silhouettes but also through the incorporation of influence from other cultures. For example, in a range of garments which depict images from the popular Amar Chitra Katha comic series, the portraits are enlarged and have large dots within them. This references their comic book origins but also draws parallels with Roy Lichtenstein's paintings and his exploration of American popular culture. The fusion of cultural influences is seen in later collections which have been much more universal; incorporating symbols such as Hokusai's wave and Samurai warriors or taking cross-cultural inspiration in themes such as the circus, the zoo, art deco façades, and futuristic cities. His trade-mark of profuse and intricate embellishment is used to its greatest and most elaborate advantage, and it is this detailed Indian craftsmanship which allows Arora to capture a universal vision of exuberance. His is a unique projection of internationalism diffused with a sense of Indian-ness.

Quotidian landscapes provide the inspiration for Little Shilpa's fashion styling, exhibits and accessories. Indian markets and street life are the spaces of everyday routines; they provide everyday items from food and spices to household goods, metal cooking vessels, plastic toys, fabric and hardware. Grounded in this daily way of life, these spaces and the objects that come from them, resonate with a common Indian identity.[57]

Facing page:
Neon deco dress.
Designed by Manish Arora.
Sequin, hand-embroidered on satin.
Autumn/Winter, 2010.
Photo courtesy Manish Arora.

76

Indicative of her imagination is the *Mumbadevi* exhibition, which was held in various locations including Lille 3000 in 2006 and at the Victoria and Albert Museum, London in 2007. Each exhibition piece resonates with a very direct sense of place. Paper cones normally used by street vendors as containers for peanuts are re-used to create a stunning head dress that descends evocatively down the wearers' back. Rangoli stickers form the decoration on a multilayered hat; plastic *jharus* (brooms) are shaped into shoulder ornaments. Other accessories are constructed from glass bangles, rubber slippers, and peacock feathers. One of the more unusual pieces is entitled 'matching centre'. The ritual of matching a piece of blouse fabric to a newly purchased sari is a familiar practice to most Indian women. Textile stalls are stocked with hundreds of fabric pieces ready cut. Shilpa's installation conveys a sense of the multitude of colour choice that is available; it invites touch, which is central to the purchase of fabric, and it is instantly recognizable to an Indian audience familiar with Indian markets. Other 'street-life' exhibition pieces include elaborate body harnesses constructed from wire and motorbike mirrors which fan out dramatically like a peacock's tail, and paper masks of Hindu gods stuck together to create elaborate head-dresses. Although these are showpieces, the Little Shilpa range also offers a diffusion line of jewellery and accessories, where the local 'finds' in a market are very much part of the global vision of the designer. Her jewellery, in which pieces of antique Indian silk and gold brocade fabric are encased between sheets of perspex, is a key example.

Although the constituents of her installation are ephemeral in nature, each has layers of meaning. The Rangoli sticker hat is linked to an older rural tradition of creating celebratory patterns on the floor using coloured powders or flower petals during the festival of Diwali. The transference of the rangoli design into the printed form of a sticker is one layer of modernity that expresses the contemporary manifestation and fluidity of tradition. Thus, the location of tradition and therefore of Indian-ness is both in the older ritual of rangoli as well as in the everyday familiarity of the market space. Through its construction into a hat, it acquires another layer of identity, a more global contemporary one. The inclusion of this hat in an exhibition which showcased the work of a 'new wave of London milliners' indicates the global nature of Shilpa's work. Her training at the London College of Fashion and subsequent apprenticeship with Philip Tracey have given her work multiple identities, at once Indian and British.[58]

Popular culture has inspired much of Nida Mahmood's work. Her earlier collections such as *High on Chai*, *New India Bioscope* and *Sadak Chhaap* reflect her interest in street life, markets, Bollywood films, street typography, and scrap. Although receiving some criticism at the time for repeating an already over-exposed kitsch aesthetic, her success in sourcing inspiration from the everyday and mundane is reflective of the great interest in this field. Her press releases express her satisfaction in making the mundane more dramatic, of taking inspiration from the simple things in life.[59] In her *Maachis* Collection she offers a more subtle but well-considered exploration of the humble matchbox. For her, matchboxes are 'small and priced at one rupee but they have the power to destroy or celebrate'.[60] The imagery, the colour palette, as well as the physical aspects of the box are incorporated into her designs. A few key motifs, such as the lotus and the bicycle, executed in different techniques of printing or embroidery, become the focal point of her range of shirts and trousers. The pattern on the rough sides of the matchboxes, the small diamond shapes of chemical and powdered glass on which you strike the match to make it light, are re-conceptualized into a variety of forms.[61] Evidence of this is seen in one of her most conspicuous outfits: a set of jodhpurs in which she repeats the bicycle motif; the stark black on white printing is then echoed in a hooded collar constructed from diamond shaped pieces of fabric which reproduce the tactility of the roughened sides of the matchbox. These diamond patterns are repeated on a range of saris; the small simple shapes, embellished with sequins, give texture and reflect light.

Within the *Maachis* Collection we can see a multi-layered construction of identity. The sense of everyday Indian-ness resonates both from the use of the Indian matchbox as inspiration and from the bicycle imagery as it reflects the common man's primary form of transport. However, rather than being a purely Indian identity, matchbox imagery, because of its own transcultural history, offers a more complex reading. The Indian match industry was heavily influenced by both the Swedish and Japanese industries and there has been much cross-cultural transportation of images, thereby leading to the popular culture of a different culture and time period being incorporated into and perceived as part of Indian popular culture.[62] Furthermore, the Jodhpur itself has a transcultural history, originating in India, derived from the churidar and becoming part of the British equestrian uniform.

Facing page:
Matchstrike outfit from Maachis Collection. Designed by Nida Mahmood. Trousers: cotton, embroidered detail. Top: cotton, origami layering. Spring/Summer 2011. Photo courtesy Nida Mahmood.

FASHION INTERNATIONALISM

A significant body of fashion designers are referencing Indian traditions in ways that are not Indian in their appearance. My Village by Rimzim Dadu and Amit Aggarwal for Morphe create western silhouettes which carry their originality in their surface textures. Their utilization of Indian resources is not through the use of handloom fabrics but through labour-intensive hand-skills which reference the Indian sensibility for embellishment and tactility. They create interesting surface textures through their manipulation of material. Rimzim's simple shift dresses are vehicles for her experimentations with textures and materials. To instil decorative interest she has developed a range of techniques which include using heat-moulded fabric to create three-dimensional effects, zip fasteners, sequins that have been burnt by hand to create colour, washers tied together with tulle. Amit Aggrawal explores forms in nature and architecture often resulting in more sculptural pieces. His incorporation of flat copper strips and complex pleating enables him to explore structure within these pieces. A series of outfits which are constructed from the insertion of different-sized discs and beads in between layers of fabric are inspired by the African tradition of scarification, creating a raised or pimpled texture. The hand-crafted nature of this work means that four skilled craftsmen take twenty hours to produce a surface of twenty square inches. The technique is a cross-cultural conversation and a contemporizing of tradition.[63]

The usual signifiers of Indian-ness are absent from the work of Kallol Datta; there is no use of recognizable craft traditions, elaborate embellishment or kitsch. This is a response to his training in London, where attempts by his tutors to make his clothes 'more Indian' through embroidery turned him in the opposite direction.[64] His work is often described in the press as grunge, anti-fit and homeless chic. However, these adjectives reduce his work to a make-shift, thrown-together, somewhat thoughtless process which masks the true ingenuity in his work – that of the construction of non-conventional silhouettes made possible though his mastery and craftsmanship in pattern-cutting which he learnt in London. His forms are draped, folded, rouched and detailed in curious ways that invite attention. His colour palette consists of black, grey, muted shades, and occasional hints of red or orange. Detailing on the garments is kept to a minimum but when used is elegantly

Facing page:
Left: 'Raised disc' dress.
Designed by Amit Aggarwal
for Morphe.
Silk, 2011.
Photo courtesy Creative Impex.

Right: 3D dress.
Designed by Rimzim Dadu for
'My Village'.
Manual 3D construction in silk
Organza, 2010.
Photo courtesy Rajesh Kashyap.

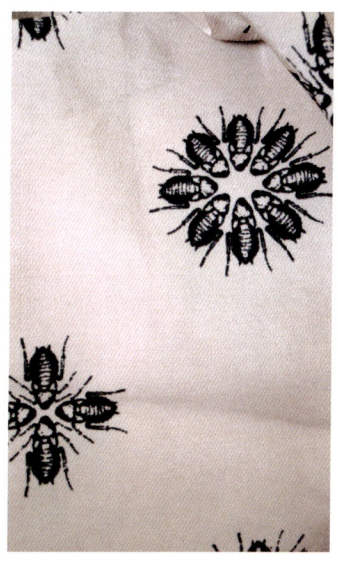

Facing page:
Landmine Series,
Mock Wrap dress.
Landmine print and outfit
by Kallol Datta.
Silk screen print.
Spring/Summer, 2010.
Photo courtesy
Kallol Datta 1955.

Above:
Left: Detail from
Infestation Series.
Roach Print by Kallol Datta.
Silk screen print.
Spring/Summer, 2010.
Photo courtesy Orla
Houston-Jibo.
Right: Detail from Dragonfly
Series on tasselled scarf.
Dragonfly print by Kallol Datta.
Silk screen print.
Spring /Summer 2010.
Photo courtesy Orla
Houston-Jibo.

done. It comes from beautifully hand-finished tassels, rope, knotting and looping. Alongside the unusual cuts, the other characteristic of his work is his prints. These are visually deceptive; they are bold and often humorous, they are aesthetically pleasing, but they unveil a shock factor. On close inspection, the floral design turns into a circle of insects, the monochrome abstract reveals a hanged man, a gentle criss-cross pattern is made from giant sperm. The prints are suitably titled 'Roadkill', 'Suicide series', 'Landmine lovers', and 'Infestation'. That these pretty motifs provoke some uncomfortable reactions is a response that Kallol has sought in his fashions. His design philosophy explores notions of conventional beauty, focusing on the more austere and less glamorous side of appearance. His clothes, which consist of dresses, baggy trousers, kurtas and shirts, are international in outlook.[65]

Craft, popular culture and internationalism have been the main routes through which fashion has been constructed during the period of this study. Dynamic and variant aesthetics encompass and convey a multiplicity of ideas pertaining to nationality, identity, modernity, and tradition. However, the nature of fashion is perpetual change, driven by social, cultural, economic, and political change, and with that comes further variations on aesthetics and further layers of meaning.

Fashion: A Visual Epilogue

The enduring vitality of the fashion industry is presented here through the work of designers who perpetuate the cosmopolitan lifestyle addressed in this book. In their imaginative adaptation of fabrics, techniques, hand skill, and machine applications, they all continue the dialogue between tradition and modernity, global and local.

क / श (KA/SHA)

Studio founded by Karishma Shahani-Khan in 2011, Pune. Fashion inspired by handcrafting and sustainability, pattern and surface embellishments, functionality, modernity, and a local-global balance.

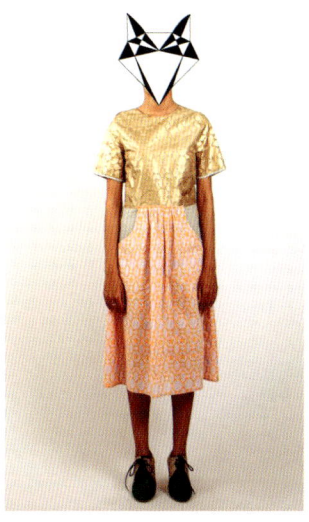

Maya, Autumn/Winter 2013.
Photographed by Wasim Khan &
Pranav Cholkar.
Photo courtesy [Ka][Sha].

Katha, Spring/Summer 2013.
Photographed by Wasim Khan &
Pranav Cholkar.
Photo courtesy [Ka][Sha].

NACHIKET BARVE

Studio founded in 2007, Mumbai. Fashion which blends India's textile heritage with an international outlook, clean simple silhouettes, intricate handcrafted techniques, and a sense of luxury.

Skirt and shirt from the Fossil
Collection.
Spring/Summer 2014.
Photo courtesy Nachiket Barve.

Romboid sari from the Hacienda
Collection.
Spring/Summer 2013.
Photo courtesy Nachiket Barve.

MANISH GUPTA

Studio founded in 2008, Delhi. Fashion that showcases simple silhouettes, embroidered embellishments with a global aesthetic.

Dress from Primrose Collection.
Spring/Summer 2013.
Photo courtesy Manish Gupta.

Dress from Primrose Collection.
Spring/Summer 2013.
Photo courtesy Manish Gupta.

PAROMITA BANERJEE

Studio founded in 2009, Kolkata. Fashion inspired by hand-woven fabrics, regional variety, and natural dyes along with aesthetic influences from Europe and Japan.

Sari, cape-style jacket.
Spring/Summer 2014.
Photo courtesy Wills Lifestyle
India Fashion Week.

Kaftan, tunic and pyjama pants.
Spring/Summer 2014.
Photo courtesy Wills Lifestyle
India Fashion Week.

PAYAL KHANDWALA

Studio founded in 2012, Mumbai. Fashion that has an Indian soul and a global aesthetic, which mixes dramatic unconventional silhouettes, asymmetric, almost architectural drapes with jewel colours, and hand-woven fabrics.

Outfit from the Sadhu and Samurai Collection.
Autumn/Winter 2012.
Photo courtesy Payal Khandwala.

Sari, waistcoat, wrap palazzo.
A Fine Balance Collection.
Autumn/Winter 2013.
Photo courtesy Payal Khandwala.

GAURAV GUPTA STUDIO

Studio founded in 2005, New Delhi. A signature look by this studio is the use of flowing fabrics and draping to create a fusion of the western evening dress and the sari.

Neon blue pink georgette sari gown with serrated shoulder 'In a Cathode'.
Spring/Summer 2013.
Photo courtesy Fashion Design Council of India.

Tangerine and pop melon georgette sari gown with multifold shoulder.
Photo courtesy Fashion Design Council of India.

89

SURENDRI

A fashion label founded by Yogesh Chaudhary in 2012, New Delhi. The label uses bold prints and bright colours to create fashions for the contemporary urban woman. Their most recognized design incorporates a graphic icon from the 1980s computer game, Pacman.

Sari from the 'Miss Pac in District' Collection.
Spring/Summer 2013.
Photo courtesy www.perniaspopupshop.com.

Outfit from the 'Miss Pac in District' Collection.
Spring/Summer 2013.
Photo courtesy www.perniaspopupshop.com.

BHANE

Online fashion brand founded in 2012 by Anand Ahuja, Delhi. Street fashion that consists of simple, comfortable, everyday basics that are youthful, fun, and style-conscious.

Couple in unisex T-shirts.
bhane.design, Fall/Winter 2013.
Photo courtesy Tenzing Dakpa.

Girl in white dress.
bhane.design, Spring/Summer 2013.
Photo courtesy Manou.

AARTI VIJAY GUPTA

Fashion studio founded in 2009, Mumbai. Inspiration for her trademark printed fabrics includes the artist's sketch book and tools as well as western fine art and music.

Dress.
'I love Music' Collection, 2013.
Photo courtesy Aarti Vijay Gupta.

Colour-wheel sari.
'I love ma doodle book'
Collection, 2012.
Photo courtesy
Aarti Vijay Gupta.

भारतीय डिज़ाइन

INDUSTRIAL DESIGN

GRAPHIC DESIGN

भारत

स्वदेशी माल

AN EXHIBITION

DESIGN IN INDIA

April 13- May 23, 1982

COMMONWEALTH INSTITUTE LONDON

GRAPHICS in INDIA

The graphic design landscape in India has in recent years seen the emergence of a range of new professional studios. They are engaging with the development of fonts, the creation of new identities, the styling of books and magazines, the digitization of indigenous graphic traditions, and other diverse and dynamic projects. Many of these studios are seeking to develop a contemporary graphic language for urban India that is based on their perception of India's changing environment, which also creates a dialogue between systems of communication, aesthetics and national identity. Their work plays an important role in the shaping of India's cosmopolitan milieus; they explore the cross-fertilization of local and global identities and strive to ensure that their graphic message communicates effectively, persuades, informs, and educates at multiple levels, within India and internationally.

DOCUMENTING GRAPHIC DESIGN

Documenting the history of graphic design was first undertaken in the 1982 exhibition, *Design in India*, held in London at the Commonwealth Institute as part of the Festival of India in Britain. At the centre of the eye-catching exhibition poster was the figure of *Bharat-mata* (Mother India), with one hand holding the Indian flag and the other placed on a pile of boxes labelled Swadeshi *mal* (Indian goods). She stood as a nationalist symbol of the early 20th-century Swadeshi movement, which promoted the boycotting of foreign goods in favour of Indian-made products. The style of the poster borrowed from a number of graphic traditions: the imagery was that of the lithographic prints of the 1930s, the medium and technique was that of the hand-painted advertising commonly seen on the streets. This multilevel visual referencing of graphic symbolism was

93

a dynamic tool with which to promote an exhibition that recognized the escalating cultural and economic force of graphic design in a developing nation. Curated by the NID, the exhibition guide is an important document of how India represented itself at a time when design was a 'young profession seeking its way'.[1] The variety of material was evidence of an active and creative design environment that was engaged with balancing social needs and commercial enterprise whilst acknowledging the vernacular.

The exhibition charted a history of the medium from the wooden printing blocks of the Kalighat pats to lithographs, posters, and labels. Newspapers such as the English language *Calcutta Chronicle* and *Modern Review* to a variety of Indian language examples including *Amrita Bazaar Patrika* (Bengali) and *Bombay Samachar* (Gujarati) were responsible for spreading literacy and encouraging social communication. The advent of advertising and the rise in print media were represented through a multitude of national magazines such as *Caravan*, *India Today*, *Star & Style* as well as local publications. Vernacular graphics and their contemporary relevance were illustrated in the form of hand-painted street signs and film hoardings. Organizations which furthered the cause of design included the Commercial Artists Group, formed in 1943, which aimed 'to make artists and designers conscious of their significance as contributors to the nation's social and economic advancement and produce the best that talents and skills can achieve'. Company logos, branding and packaging illustrated modern graphic development, with particularly successful examples cited as Mukund Steel, Indian Diary Corporation, Hindustan Petroleum, and Air India. Conveying the broader definition of graphic design was the inclusion of a section under the heading of *Design for Need* which focused on its utilitarian function in relation to maps, signage and the creation of type-forms for India's national language, whilst also raising the challenge of designing a common script for fifteen of India's languages. Thirty years later the potential for graphic design to enhance communication across these various functions has still to be fully realized. The NID remains one of the few institutions to spearhead projects that contribute to civic needs as seen in the re-designing of the national census forms for 2011, a phenomenally detailed and painstaking exercise undertaken by Rupesh Vyas.[2]

Today, graphic design is even more prevalent not only through the proliferation of printed matter but also with the advancement of

Facing page:
Panel from Design in India exhibition. Designed by the National Institute of Design, Ahmedabad, 1982. Photo courtesy National Institute of Design.

AN IMAGE OF EXCELLENCE

A SPECIAL
EXUBERANCE

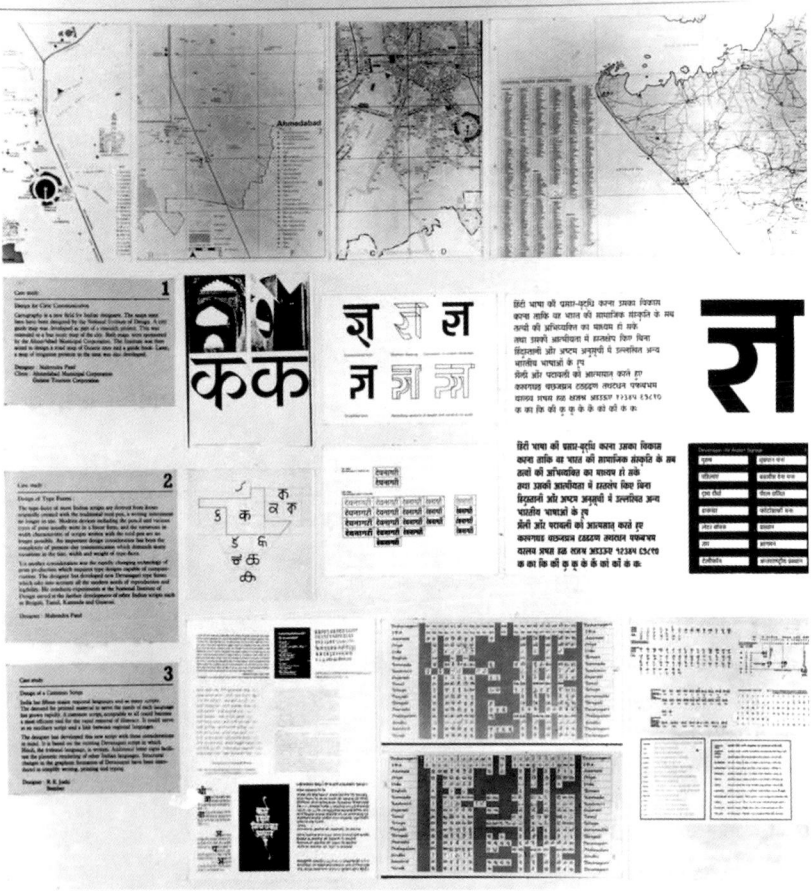

Panel from Design in India
exhibition.
Designed by the National
Institute of Design,
Ahmedabad, 1982.
Photo courtesy National
Institute of Design.

technology and the arrival of the internet. Globalization and technology
have had a fundamental impact on the practice, production, and
consumption of graphic design. Digitization and software programmes
allow infinite manipulation and layering of text and picture, framing,
colour, size, and scale. This increased flexibility enables designers to
realize their ideas in faster and cheaper ways.[3] Geoffrey Caban in his
overview of contemporary graphic design across the non-western
world notes that: 'It is difficult to find examples of visual communication
that have not been touched in some way by new technologies and

international design approaches,' which is a result of the designer's often cross-continental education, travel, and exposure to the world through a variety of media. However, these designers are also very aware of and influenced by their indigenous traditions.[4] The studios and projects examined here reflect these dialogues. Their work stands in contrast to the vast majority of graphic design in India, which is produced by Desktop Publishing companies where 'design' is the product of software programmes and DTP operators. The professionally trained and better informed studios discussed here have been selected because they create a particular visual environment within the metropolitan centres; one that is expressed and experienced through a limited range of popular graphic genres. Their aesthetic choices are an expression of local and global identities. Most wish to avoid graphic treatments that project over-exposed versions of Indian-ness as seen, for example, in Bollywood-style typography; some choose to utilize a minimal and clean aesthetic; others employ colour, pattern, and motifs that reference a variety of Indian traditions. In documenting their objectives and concerns, this study captures a snapshot of the graphic landscape over a brief but significant period of time, for future design historians to reference and re-evaluate.

TERMS OF REFERENCE

Newark defines the function of graphic designers today as being one of 'making sense and creating difference'; in other words, 'giving order and structure to enable better communication and to do that in a unique way'.[5] Graphic design combines text and image, art and technology, to communicate effectively as well as provide a visual experience. As a design discipline it includes the individual fields of typography, printing, advertising, illustration, and photography. Typography refers to the placement of letterforms on a page, from an individual letter to a word, line, column, margin and so forth. It involves making decisions about the typeface (the form of the letter), the font (the full set of letters, numbers, size, bold, italic), the space surrounding the type, and the rhythmic balance of the whole. Apart from providing a structure, typography can also be associative, reflecting the ideas within the text. Image-making involves the use of illustration and photography. Graphic design decisions also consider the materiality of the object, what it is printed on, made of, its scale and tactility. Style refers to the overall look of the piece.[6]

BOMBAY ELECTRIC

Signage for Bombay Electric, Mumbai.
Designed by Priya Kishore and Miki
Amano, 2006.
Photo courtesy Bombay Electric.

Clothing label for Bombay
Electric, Mumbai.
Designed by Priya Kishore and
Miki Amano, 2006.
Photo courtesy Bombay Electric.

The BUNGALOW

..n, designed by
...ithli Ahluwalia.
..e drama lies in
..theatrics, the
..luminous yet
..global.
..Parisian precision and a grunge-
..ous nonchalance with handcrafted shiboris,
brocades, khadis, ikkats and aging embroideries. In every
garment, there is always that unexpected detail that pushes
the label into a hitherto unseen realm of fashion.

Label for Bungalow 8, Mumbai.
Identity designed by
Vishal Rawley.
Stamp format designed by
Lokesh Karekar of Locopopo,
2003/2011.
Photo courtesy Bunglow 8
and Lokesh Karekar.

GRAPHIC IDENTITY AND THE ENVIRONMENT

India's cosmopolitan environments are constructed and experienced through graphic design interfaces such as shop signage, restaurant menus, packaging, retail and print advertising, as well as websites. Examined here is a small selection of examples which demonstrate how graphic design uses style to convey the nature and content of a space. The fashion boutique, Bombay Electric, known for its chic contemporary clothing, uses for its logo a typeface composed of little black stars on a white background to transmit the vibrancy or 'electricity' of the city. It was inspired by a photograph of the floodlights at Mumbai's Wankhade Stadium taken by Priya Kishore, the owner of the store, and translated into a graphic form by Miki Amano, a Japanese graphic designer.[7] Located in the same area is Bungalow 8, a store known for its eclectic mix of interior products, fashion, and jewellery. Based in a converted heritage property, the stylish décor juxtaposes the old and new, with exposed walls, distressed painted wood and polished cement. Their graphic identity consists of the splitting in half of the letter B and number 8 and their re-configuration

99

Founded in 2003, pioneering concept store Bungalow 8 has always been something of a retail enigma. Its uncompromising vision, unconventional locations, avant-garde interiors and lived-in displays catalyzed the coming of age of Global-Indian design. It has charmed the international style cognoscenti, is often mentioned by leading design magazines such as Wallpaper as one of the best stores in the world, and has music legends like Madonna and Sting, and design icons like Patricia Urquiola and Tricia Guild, among its clients.

In true Bungalow 8 tradition, there is little to suggest that this is a retail store. It could just as well be the home of a grande dame, comfortable straddling the past and present. Both the interiors and fashion selections are curated with finesse and flair, and range from vintage furniture, tableware, linen, decorative accessories and sculpture to garments, scarves, bags and jewelry. An absolute must visit for the design-conscious.

BUNGALOW EIGHT
8
INTERIORS · FASHION

PLACE
STAMP
HERE

Grants Building, 1st, 2nd and 3rd floors, 17 Arthur Bunder Road, Colaba, Mumbai - 400005
T: +91 22 22819880/1/2 E: contact@bungaloweight.com W: www.bungaloweight.com

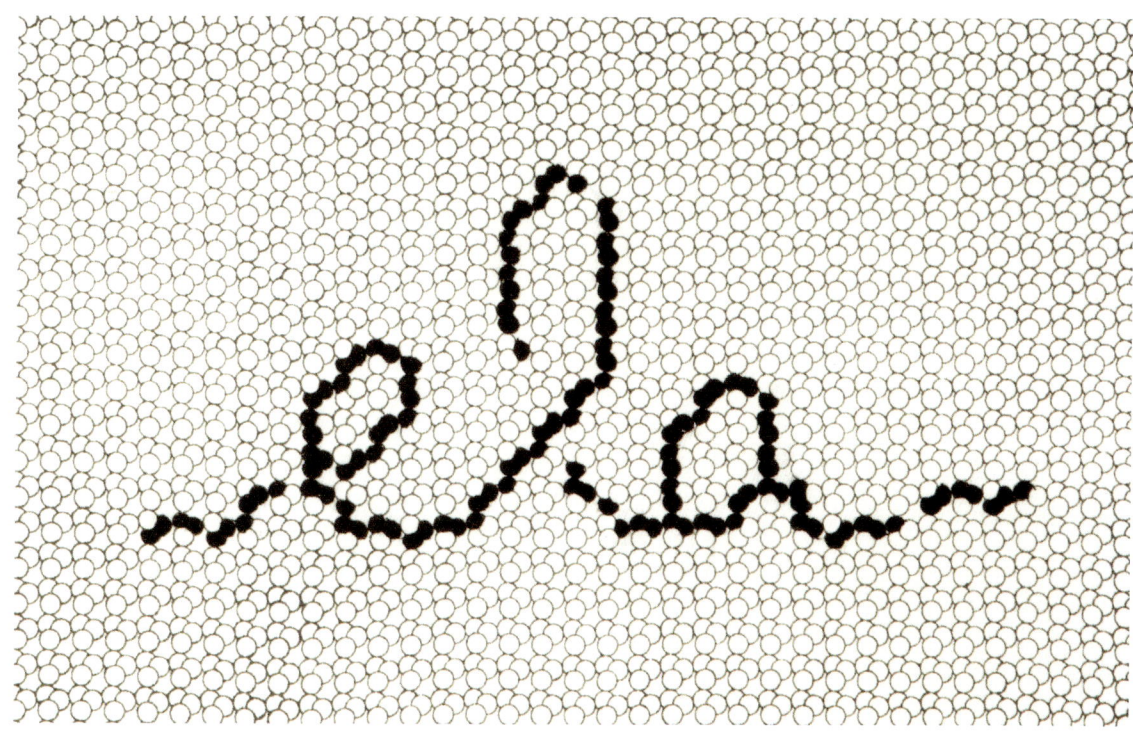

Facing page:
Postcard for Bungalow 8,
Mumbai.
Designed by Lokesh Karekar
of Locopopo, 2011.
Photo courtesy Bunglow 8
and Lokesh Karekar.

Above:
Logo Design for Ela, an haute
couture line of organic wear
for women.
Designed by Ishan Khosla
Design, 2010.
Photo courtesy Ishan
Khosla Design.

into one bold symbol. Designed by Vishal Rawley, it conveys the dualities of the local and global, of heritage and contemporary which underpin the ethos of the store. A recent commission to convert the logo into a format for use on labels and other printed material saw graphic designer Lokesh Karekar transfer the symbol onto an old-fashioned embossing hand-stamp. The same aesthetic and commercial message is conveyed on postcards distributed throughout the store.[8] Encounters with graphic design in this setting continue with labels inside clothing. Ela, a fashion brand working with 100 per cent organic cotton and stocked in Bombay Electric and other specialist stores, has a distinct logo created by Ishan Khosla Design. Here, we see a form of visual onomatopoeia, the effect being one that exudes a sense of organic-ness; a circular grid allows a fluid, unstructured development of letterforms that, when produced in contrasting black and white, project a simple but striking effect.[9]

Restaurants are also a significant part of this urban culture. The importation of international cuisines, for example, has led to the demand for a relevant and corresponding graphic style. An interesting case study is the graphic identity for Olive, a Mediterranean restaurant

olive
BAR & KITCHEN

on the turf

INDIGO

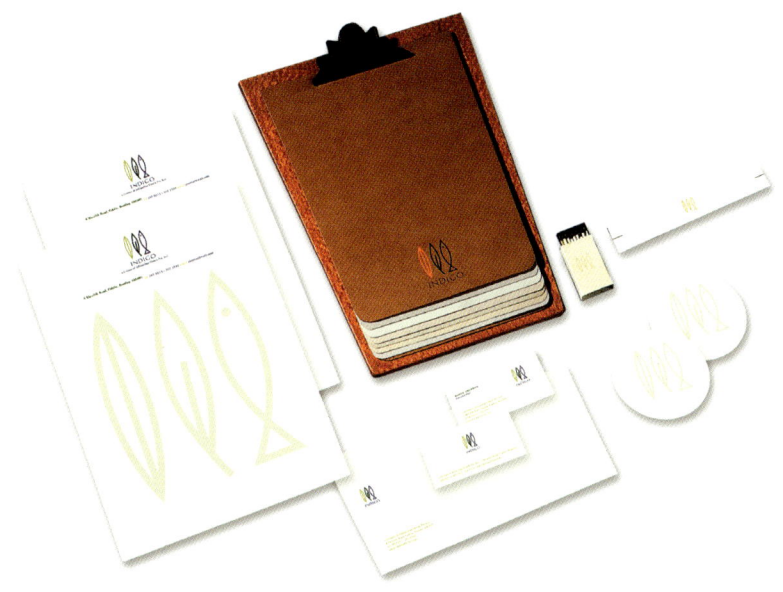

Facing page:
Top: Identity for Olive
Restaurant, Mumbai.
Designed by Grandmother
India, 2000.
Photo courtesy
Grandmother India.
Centre: Identity for Tote
on the Turf, Mumbai.
Designed by Design
Temple, 2011.
Photo courtesy Design Temple.
Below: Identity for Indigo.
Designed by Itu Chaudhuri
Design, 1999.
Photo courtesy
Itu Chaudhuri Design.

Above:
Design Menu and stationery
for Indigo, Mumbai.
Designed by Itu Chaudhuri
Design, 1999.
Photo courtesy
Itu Chaudhuri Design.

in Mumbai. It links the simultaneous development of the design studio, Grandmother India, started in 1999 by Kurnal Rawat and Tejas Mangeshkar, with that of the restaurant, opened in 2000, to the border cosmopolitan cultural milieu of the time: 'Olive wanted to be stylish and iconic from day one… We nurtured the Olive Brand from the start, and the work we did on Olive helped define not only the restaurant's identity but ours as well'.[10] The aesthetic inspiration came from the rural Mediterranean use of stark whitewash stucco walls, simple expressive brush strokes and a limited colour palette. Another example is Indigo, also launched in 1999; as a modern European restaurant, it offers simplicity and fine ingredients in its cooking. The identity, designed by Itu Chaudhuri Design, conveys this through the paring down of three key ingredients into simple line-drawn icons representing a single rice grain, a fish, and a leaf.[11] In contrast, the logo for Tote on the Turf does not express the nature of the food but cleverly references the past history of the building as a counting house for horse-racing bets. Design Temple have created a graphic identity that stylistically suggests subtraction and addition symbols within the lettering and reflects the strong architectural identity of Serie Architect's restaurant design.

As a reflection of its persuasive and ubiquitous nature, graphic design enables the lifestyle projected by these restaurants to be taken home

through the branded products sold within these spaces. Turning Point wine, for example, with packaging designed by Design Temple, is marketed to a young urban group and sold in Indigo deli, part of the Indigo chain. The bottles are shrink-wrapped in silver with a pattern inspired by Op-Art which is geometric, trendy, and executed in very contemporary colours. Chaitime, a range of speciality teas also sold in similar spaces, has been packaged with a graphic treatment by Alok Nanda & Company, which gives a visually global appeal to a local drink. A parallel narrative is offered through the designing and re-designing of identities for some of India's major household brands. The need for these brands to communicate their responsiveness to the increasingly cosmopolitan environment and to maintain and expand consumers both nationally and internationally is articulated through the replacement of cluttered detailing with simplified clarity. Two renowned brand design agencies are responsible for some notable examples; these include Ray+Keshavan's work for Infosys and Bank of Baroda, as well as Elephant Design's identities for Godrej and Bajaj.

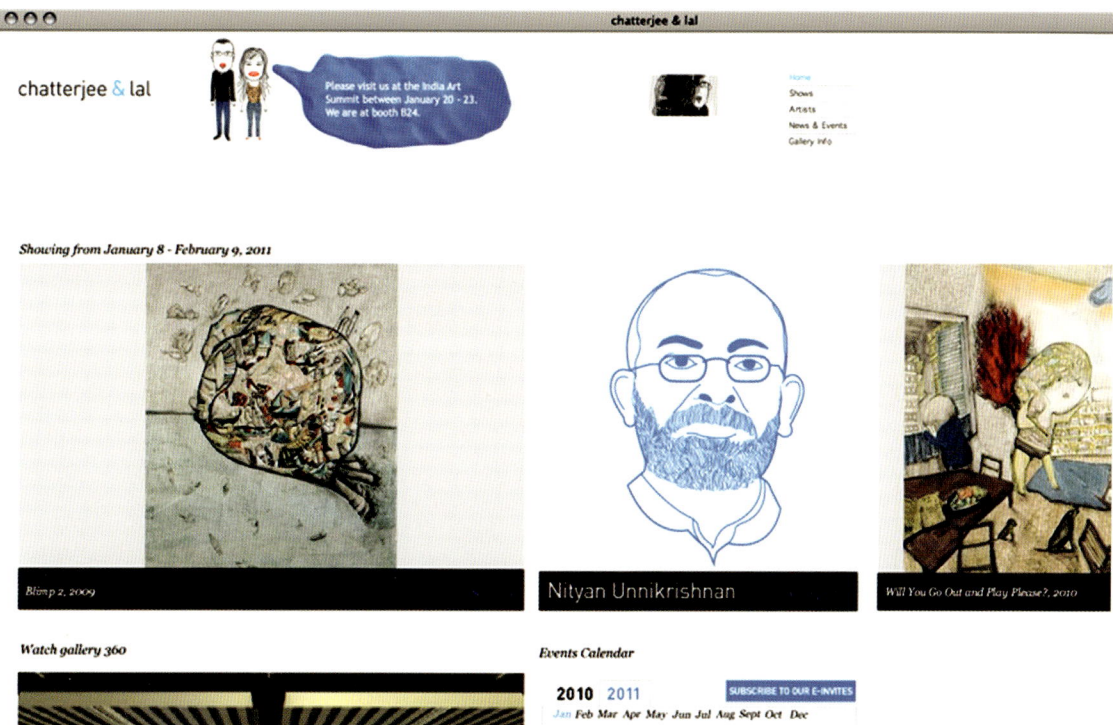

Identity and digital design for Chatterjee and Lal. Designed by Design Stack, 2010. Photo courtesy Design Stack.

Another feature of the cosmopolitan environment is the contemporary art gallery, an interesting example being Chatterjee and Lal, founded in 2003. Their graphic identity, as seen on their cards, stationery and through their website, has been realized by Design Stack, Mumbai. It is unusual in that it uses an illustration of the two gallery owners. Young and increasingly visible on the art scene, they are the best advertisements for their gallery. The quirky colour illustration injects a sense of humour, bringing some informality back to art and helping to diminish its high-brow attitude. The image, set on a white background with a very simple clean typeface, reflects the individuality of a company that has a reputation for showcasing more avant-garde artists.[12] Central to all the examples of graphic identity documented here is a desire to effectively and creatively communicate the contemporary and unique nature of the enterprise.

105

INDIA **NOW** | V&A

The Visual Language of New India

Like any work of art, the design repertoire of India is linked to the historical period and the society in which it was created.

Over the centuries it has had a variety of external and internal influences; from the early Greco-Roman styles of the Gandhara period (second to fourth century A.D.) to the geometric motifs, domes, minarets of the Indo-Islamic Mughal period (sixteenth to eighteenth century AD) through to the fusion of Indo-European designs of the chintz trade (seventeenth to nineteenth century).

The idea of hybrids and collaborative work created for use within India or for different parts of the world is not new to Indian design.

However, today, India's rapid growth has resulted in the blind replication of the 'urban, Western look', creating 'modern' buildings, shopping malls, homes, advertising and mass communication that threaten to change the landscape of the cities we live in.

This is where, we hope, the birth of contemporary Indian design can play a role in preserving Indian identity. New designers are exploring India's heritage, its crafts and technologies and producing products, graphics, fashion and more, in an indigenous design language that has global relevance.

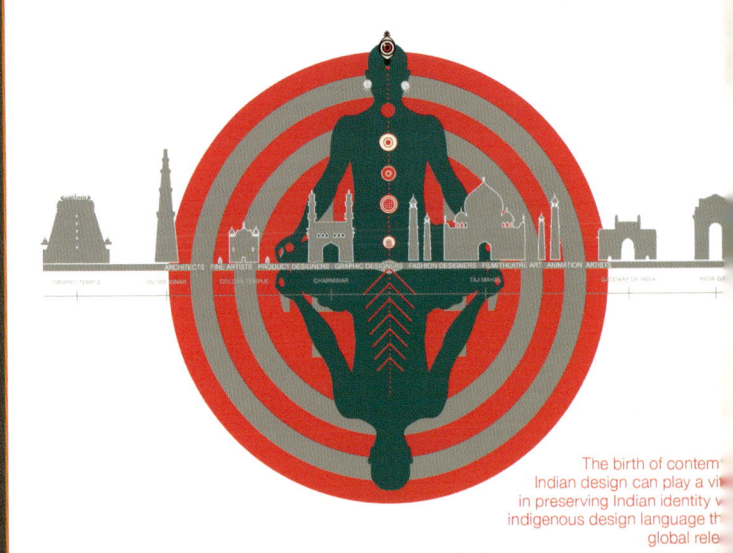

The birth of contem
Indian design can play a vi
in preserving Indian identity v
indigenous design language th
global rele

106

DESIGN-CULTURE GRAPHICS

Adrian Shaughnessey recorded, in 2005, that alongside the traditional mainstream function of graphic design as a communicator of information there has been the emergence of 'design-culture graphics'. This was manifested through the rise of small groups and individuals who produced magazines, websites, and items of graphic paraphernalia such as T-shirts and posters with a 'new more radical and adventurous style'. These are often self-initiated catering for a new market, that of the 'follower of the cult of design'. Furthermore, as these are featured and reproduced in books about style, they have developed their own currency in raising profile. Thus he concludes that graphic design has stopped being a discipline and has become a culture.[13]

This is a trend that has manifested itself in India and highlights the on-going debates about style over substance. Emphasis on style suggests a shift away from the 'true' function of graphic design, reducing its problem solving, communication, and organising functions to pointless ephemera. However, all graphic forms have a style: whether it is a railway ticket or a magazine, the aesthetic of it is a reflection of the period in which it was produced, conveying the economic, social, and political concerns of the time. Culture can be expressed and understood through style.[14] Scott Minick and Jiao Ping's exploration of Chinese graphic design in the 20th century for example, charts a chronological shift into successive decades, discussing the graphic styles in their social and political context, from the Art Deco influenced Shanghai Style, to the national design style influenced by Russian Constructivism, to the search for a new identity as seen in the late 1980s.[15] Studies of Indian film graphics have taken an art historical approach, documenting from the earliest text-based leaflets to the influence of western academic painting, through to the use of computer-generated imagery, placing them within their social and cultural context.[16] The stylistic considerations of the group of designers discussed here will therefore play their part in the story of graphic design in India.

Design Temple and Play Clan are two studios at the heart of the evolution of 'design-culture graphics'. They share similarities in their development trajectories and a *raison d'être* to create a design identity for a new urban context. Both gather their inspiration from India, observing histories and respecting local and national cultures within a

Panel for India Now display at V&A Museum, London. Designed by Design Temple, 2007. Photo courtesy Design Temple.

107

globalizing environment. Their graphic sensibility has been projected into an ever-increasing range of 'designer' products that are sold through their own outlets as well as other design-friendly retail spaces. Both have a strong sense of their identity based on their particular philosophy through which they have developed their unique styles.

Design Temple was launched in 2000, responding to the changing post-liberalization environment. Founded by Divya Thakur, the company has engaged with graphic design as identity creation, as communication and as art with a primary aim of developing an urban Indian design language. This derives from a desire to counteract excessive westernisation. One of their first projects was to create an identity for Le Vie Dell' Oriente which entailed presenting a modern identity for India and Asia to the Italian business community. This forced an engagement with western perceptions of India and India's perceptions of itself. Such questioning helped hone the company's design philosophy: to link the past to the present and to create and communicate with global relevance. For Design Temple 'global relevance' does not imply a break away from India, but rather to 'belong more'.[17]

In 2007, commissioned by the Victoria and Albert Museum to create an installation entitled *India Now* that conveyed their perception of India at the cusp of change, they expressed the need for contemporary design to fully realize its role in preserving a national identity. Their graphic panels were a showcase for their 'indigenous design language with a global relevance' where their newly designed symbols representing the Indian home, fashion, food, and the IT industry illustrated Indian customs in a clean, stylized, and elegant manner.[18] Their Indian design language has mainly evolved through their products. The initial range released in 2006 consisted of quirky items that were an outlet for their creativity and a testing of the market place. Products such as matchboxes, incense-stick packets, and diary planners also sell the concept of 'contemporary Indian design' as applied to common, everyday items. They are a lifestyle choice catering to a young urban, creative, upwardly mobile group. Their *Mantra Matchboxes* and *Holy Smoke* incense-sticks are acquired not purely for their function but also for their appealing contemporary and chic packaging, which conveys a very clear mix of local visual language and global production values. The matchbox covers use the concept of metaphoric type, where letterforms are used to shape an image that represents the message being conveyed.

Facing page:
Left: Holy Smoke incense sticks. Designed by Design Temple, 2011. Photo courtesy Design Temple.

Right: Mantra Matchboxes. Designed by Design Temple, 2011. Photo courtesy Design Temple.

109

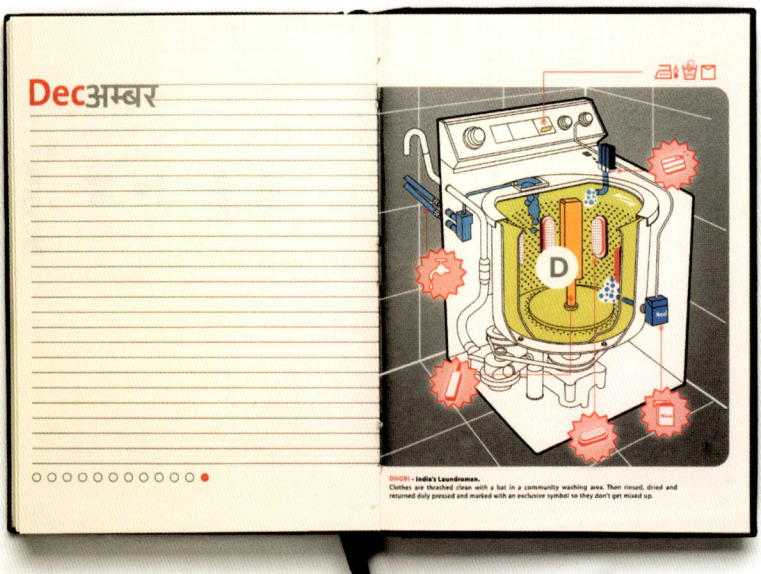

Above: Autorickshaw.
Page from Parrot Diary.
Designed by Design Temple, 2009.
Photo courtesy V&A Museum, London

Below: Dhobi.
Page from Parrot Diary.
Designed by Design Temple, 2009.
Photo courtesy V&A Museum, London.

Their most iconic products include the Parrot Diaries, which incorporate clever pictograms and detailed illustrations. The first of the range, released in 2007, was themed the 'A-Z of Indian cool' and re-visualized common Indian objects and processes such as the rickshaw or tea-drinking. Subsequent themes such as *Hindustan Hipsters* and *Erogenius* re-work the very clichéd visual representations of Indian spirituality and the Kama Sutra into elegant, contemporary graphic forms. Examined as a whole, the visual grammar that Design Temple have developed manages to balance the ornate with the understated, the elegant with the quirky to create what Divya Thakur describes as 'European simplicity and mastery of machine with India's vibrancy and ancient heritage'. Client-based work has also helped to establish their reputation; this has included the designing of books, visual identities for companies, signage systems, and websites. The range of products has recently grown to include fashion, furniture, lighting, ceramics, and graphic art; the re-positioning of the studio allows a broader canvas on which to apply the studio's distinct visual language.

Offering a different aesthetic but a similar ethos is Play Clan, a Delhi-based company launched by Himanshu Dogra that started to 'evolve, create and play' in 2008 and claim a 'fresh, alternate, anti-ordinary love for India'.[19] They have created their own cult of design through the construction of an imaginary alternative universe, the 'Republic of Play Clan', inhabited by square-brained clones that are mischievous, stylish and fun-seeking by nature. The concept of the clan offers endless possibilities for extension: consumers are encouraged to join and adopt clan identities; the Republic releases public notices announcing new collections, collaborations and events; opening stores in other cities becomes a process of 'Clonization' by the Republic where like-minded people can become part of the clan colony.

The best example of their graphic treatment is through their postings on Facebook.[20] The square-brained clones have been depicted with small bodies and oversized square heads and they comment on topical issues and occasionally appear as a variety of characters from popular culture such as James Bond. They mark nation-wide annual celebrations and notable birthdays or anniversaries and release 'weekly wisdom' postcards which offer wise thoughts. The image and text combine to create a bold and dynamic graphic style, colourful

Above: Vastu Shastra.
Page from Parrot Diary.
Designed by Design Temple, 2009.
Photo courtesy V&A Museum, London.

Below: Chai/Tea.
Page from Parrot Diary.
Designed by Design Temple, 2007.
Photo courtesy V&A Museum, London.

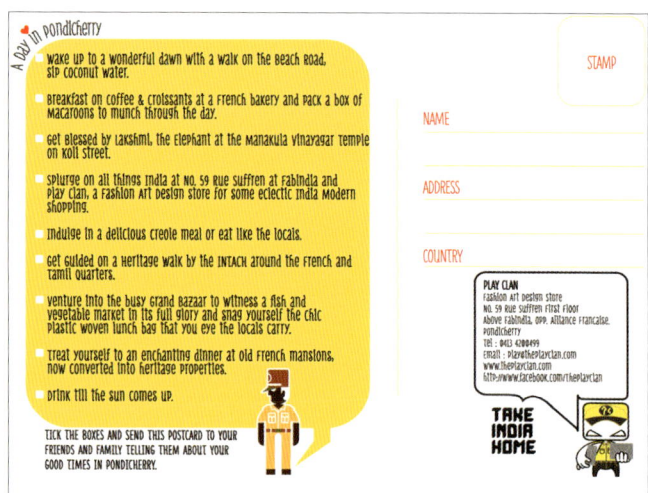

with humorous imagery. A narrative woven around clone characters conveys the philosophy of 'transforming the mundane into magic', which is experienced through their website, social media pages, and their products. The narrative also takes the clones on journeys through Delhi, Mumbai, Jodhpur, Pondicherry, and Kochi, with the products themed accordingly to their observations of the local culture within these cities; the re-working of cultural icons such as a kathakali dancer or a Mumbai fisher woman being reflective of this. While the clones create this fun-filled universe, they do not appear on most of the products; rather the products are embedded with their ethos but work independently of them, giving them a longer lifespan and a broader consumer appeal. Play Clan have created an unmistakable aesthetic, one defined by colour, vibrancy and sense of fun, with a more delicate and detailed quality to their illustration. Clients and collaborators commission them because of their distinct graphic language, examples of which include the 'hip city guide' for *Elle* magazine and their installations at Wills Fashion Week 2011, and Mela at India Design Forum 2012.[21]

Illustration for 'Something
Relevant', album cover for
Mumbai based indie-jazz band.
Illustration by Sameer Kulavoor
of Bombay Duck Design, 2009.
Photo courtesy Sameer
Kulavoor.

While Design Temple and Play Clan represent well-established,
larger-scale studios, Locopopo, run by Lokesh Karekar, and Bombay
Duck Designs, run by Sameer Kulavoor, are examples of smaller, edgier
studios, their work reflective of a younger cutting-edge experimental
stage in their career trajectory.[22] In keeping with the characteristics
of 'design-culture graphics' they convey an aesthetic that is often in
opposition or 'radical' to that which surrounds it and they too produce
paraphernalia. For both studios the city of Mumbai holds a deep
fascination and this is manifested through commercial and personal
projects. Both have produced a series of limited-edition prints with
Locopopo focusing on icons of south Mumbai, and Bombay Duck

Designs, on the bicycle-wallahs of the city. Client commissions often request illustrations of the city, as seen in *GQ Magazine* and *Mumbai Boss*. For Kulavoor, this has engaged him in a series of projects from *Love Bombay*, a city guide, and Kyani café, a personal exploration of a Mumbai institution, to the album-cover design for the band Something Relevant and the animation for the music video *Lovedrug Climbdown* by Pentagram. The latter captures the feeling of the city, where, according to Pentagram's website, there is a 'growing, throbbing, suddenly self-aware "scene" in Bombay... and across the major cities of India... There is, and has been for a few years now, a very self-reliant, very vibrant "indie" element to urban thought in India, one that finds

115

Thurs 5th Feb 03
at Rock Bottom

BHAVISHYAVANI
Fast dancing for a new India

BREAKBEAT / NU SKOOL BREAKZ
MANEESH THE TWISTER   INSAT   KUTKLASS
(Dhamaal, San Francisco)

10 PM ONWARDS
Club Rules Apply

ROCK

Poster for Bhavishyavani
at Rock Bottom.
Designed by
BHA Design Co, 2003.
Photo courtesy
BHA Design Co.

Facing page:
Poster for Bhavishyavani
at Blue Frog.
Designed by
BHA Design Co, 2008.
Photo courtesy
BHA Design Co.

expression through art, through cultural activity, and of course, through music. It's the unique voice of urban India, which is raring to break the bounds of the conventional concept of India known across the world'.[23] This statement resonates because these graphic design projects are part of that stimulating urban sensibility. At the heart of the underground music scene in Mumbai is Bhavishyavani, a music events agency. Launched in 1999, it was the first to showcase cutting-edge global and local music trends to a young eager audience. The tagline 'Fast dancing for a new India' used on their promotional material captured the youthful energy and creative spirit of the time. Designed by BHA Design Co, the leaflets and posters reference technology and connectivity.

One of BHA Design Co's first graphic explorations for Bhavishyavani was with the map of Mumbai in which they played with the grid lines, rearranging them and distorting the sectors while directing people to the location of the event. Mapping Mumbai is a favourite tool of graphic

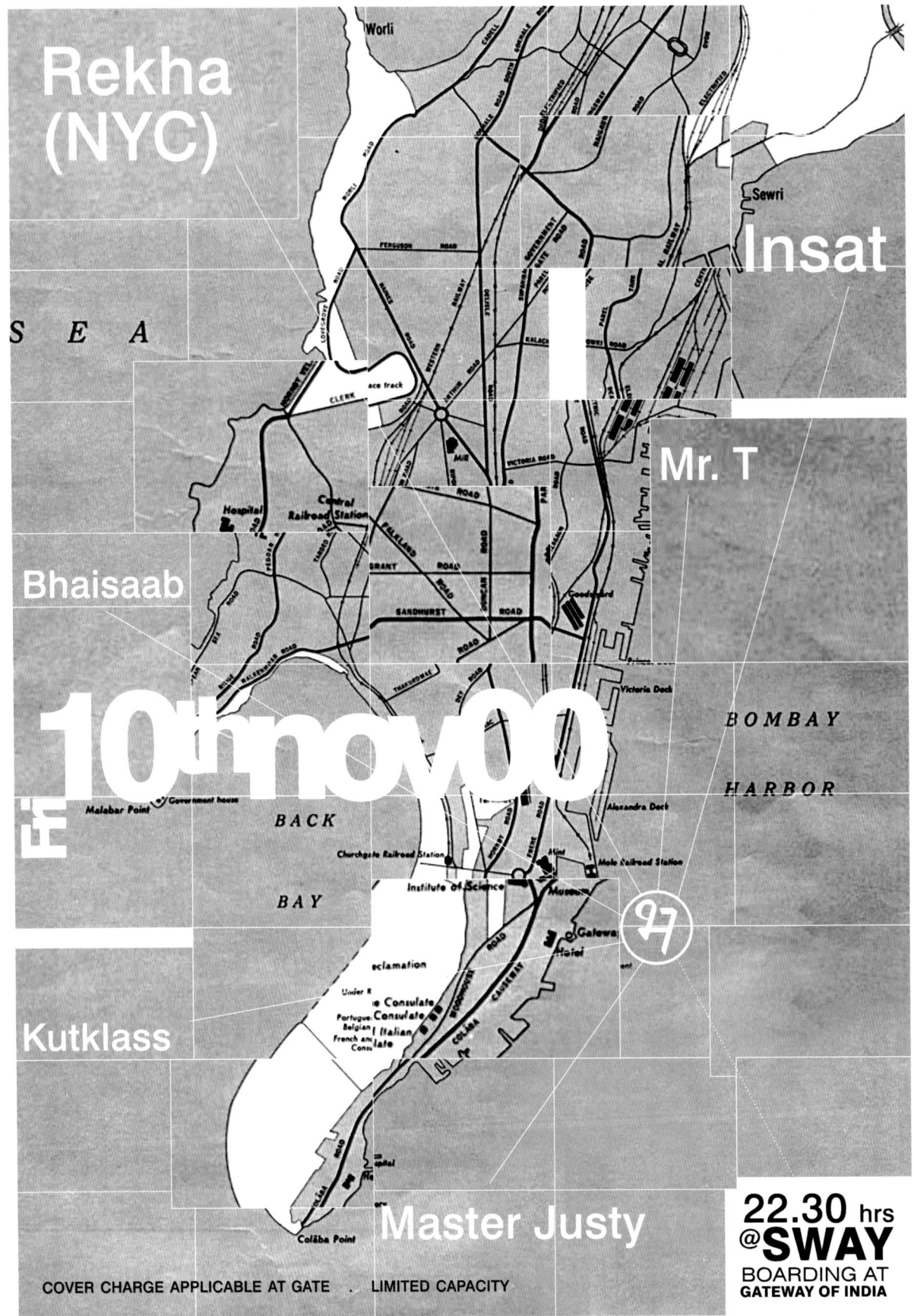

Rekha
(NYC)

Insat

Mr. T

Bhaisaab

Fri 10th nov00

Kutklass

Master Justy

COVER CHARGE APPLICABLE AT GATE . LIMITED CAPACITY

22.30 hrs
@SWAY
BOARDING AT
GATEWAY OF INDIA

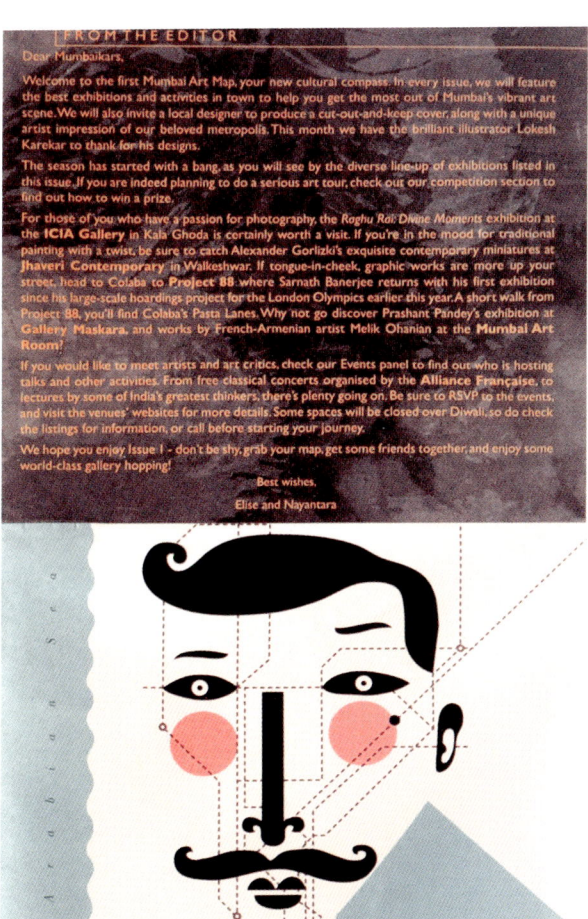

Facing page:
Poster for Bhavishyavani
at SWAY.
Designed by BHA Design Co,
2000.
Photo courtesy
BHA Design Co.

Above:
Mumbai Boss map.
Illustration by Lokesh Karekar
of Locopopo, 2012.
Photo courtesy Lokesh Karekar.

Following pages:
Mapping Mumbai's intersections.
Designed by Shilpa
Chavan, 2007.
Photo courtesy Shilpa Chavan.

designers: several interpretations are offered in the catalogue for Shilpa Chavan's *Mumbadevi* fashion installation.[24] Each map represents a different aspect of the city; the two most striking examples employ the power of typography. One marks the stalls and streets of the Chor Bazaar using only words which describe the merchandise category of the stalls; the other is a typographic mimicking of the major roundabouts and intersections in the city. Locopopo's Mumbai City Map was commissioned by the newspaper *Mumbai Boss* to locate the city's art exhibitions during the October to December season 2012. The graphic interpretation is endearingly called the 'Mumbai-map moustache man' and is a visualization of the map of Mumbai as seen through the overlay of the proposed new public transport routes for the forthcoming mono-rail system. The face is an extremely dynamic, often used graphic tool which engages the viewer's eye and commands attention. Here, the face of a chiselled-cheekboned, man-about-town is created using the grid

119

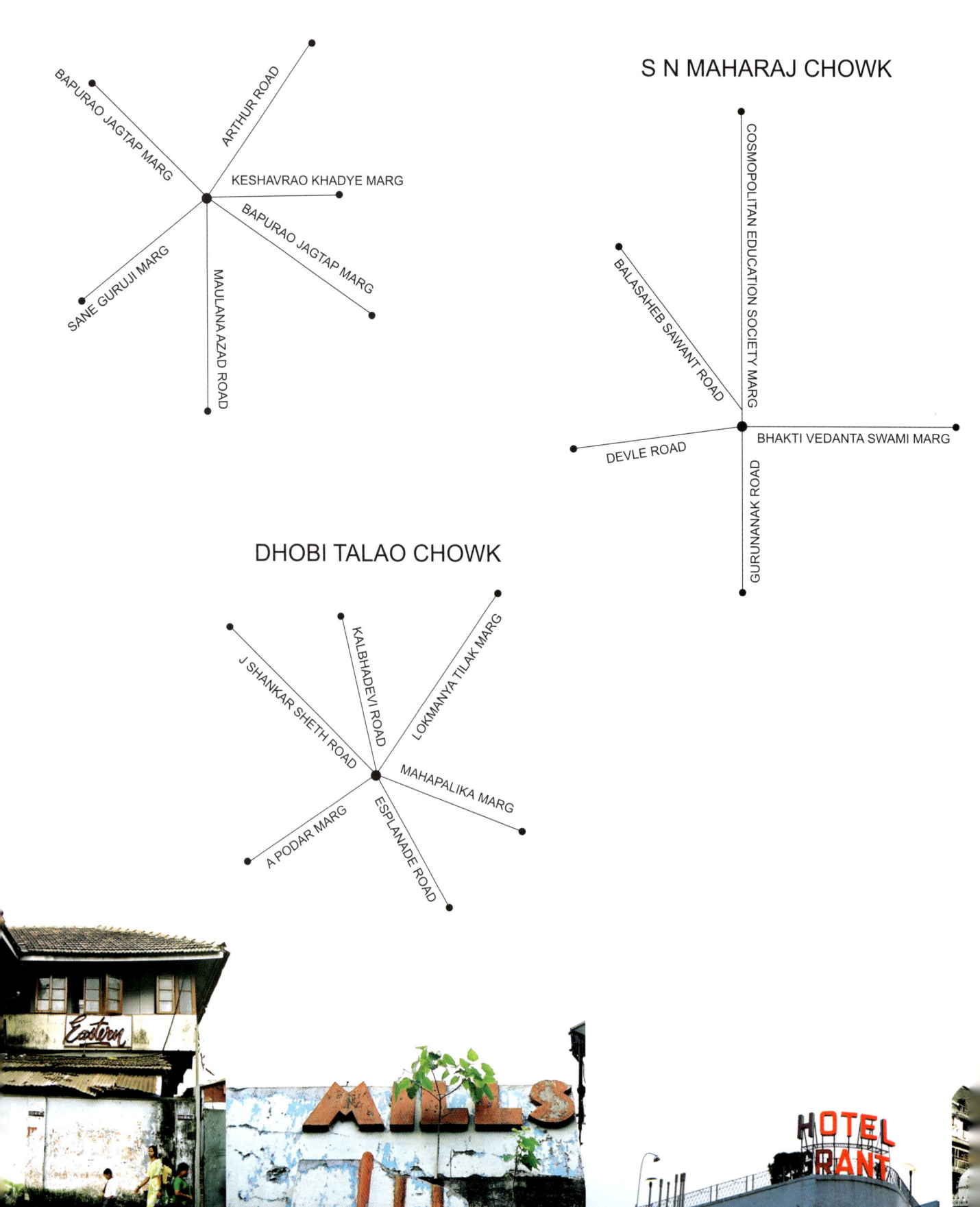

JACOB CIRCLE

BAPURAO JAGTAP MARG

ARTHUR ROAD

KESHAVRAO KHADYE MARG

BAPURAO JAGTAP MARG

SANE GURUJI MARG

MAULANA AZAD ROAD

S N MAHARAJ CHOWK

COSMOPOLITAN EDUCATION SOCIETY MARG

BALASAHEB SAWANT ROAD

DEVLE ROAD

BHAKTI VEDANTA SWAMI MARG

GURUNANAK ROAD

DHOBI TALAO CHOWK

J SHANKAR SHETH ROAD

KALBHADEVI ROAD

LOKMANYA TILAK MARG

MAHAPALIKA MARG

A PODAR MARG

ESPLANADE ROAD

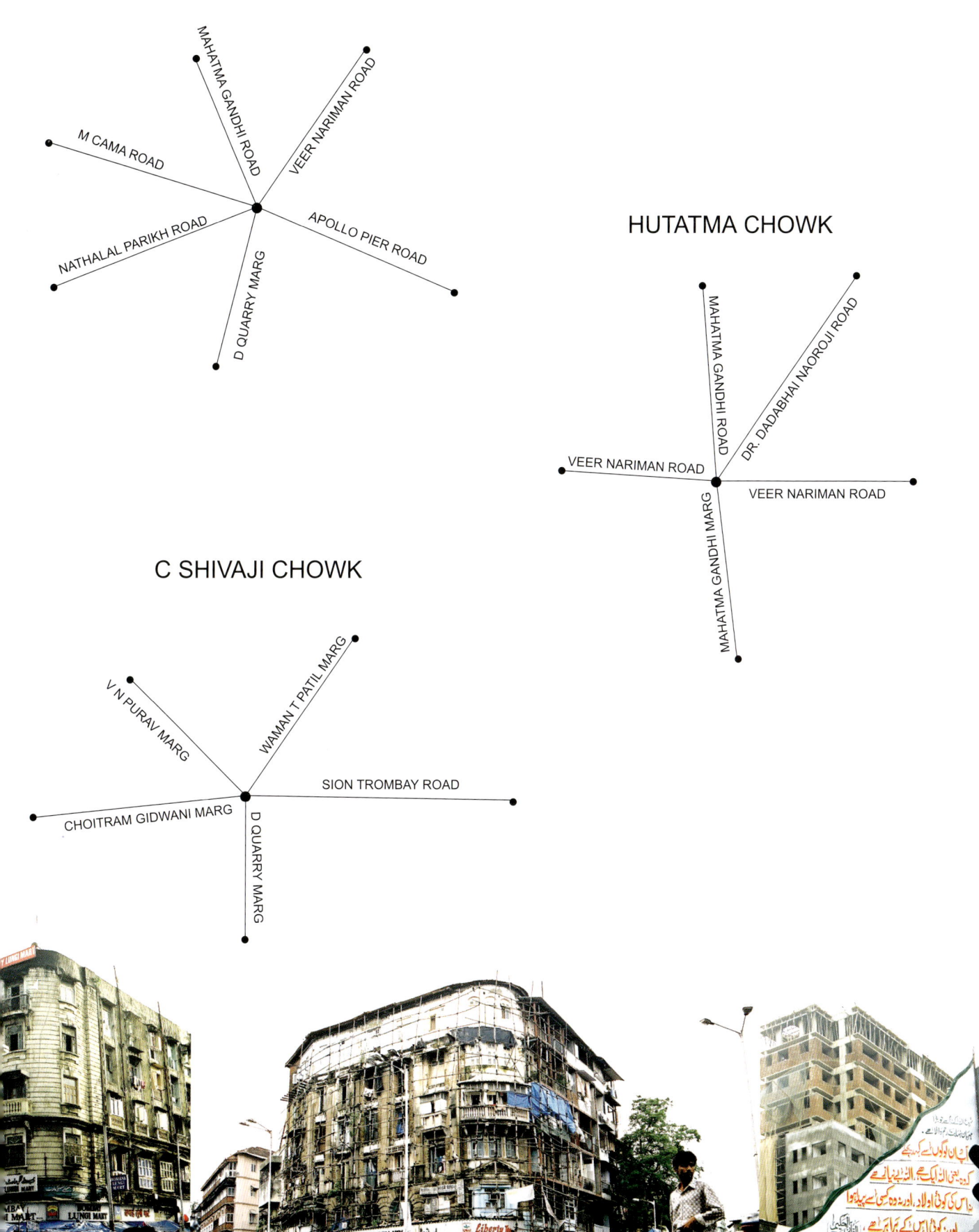

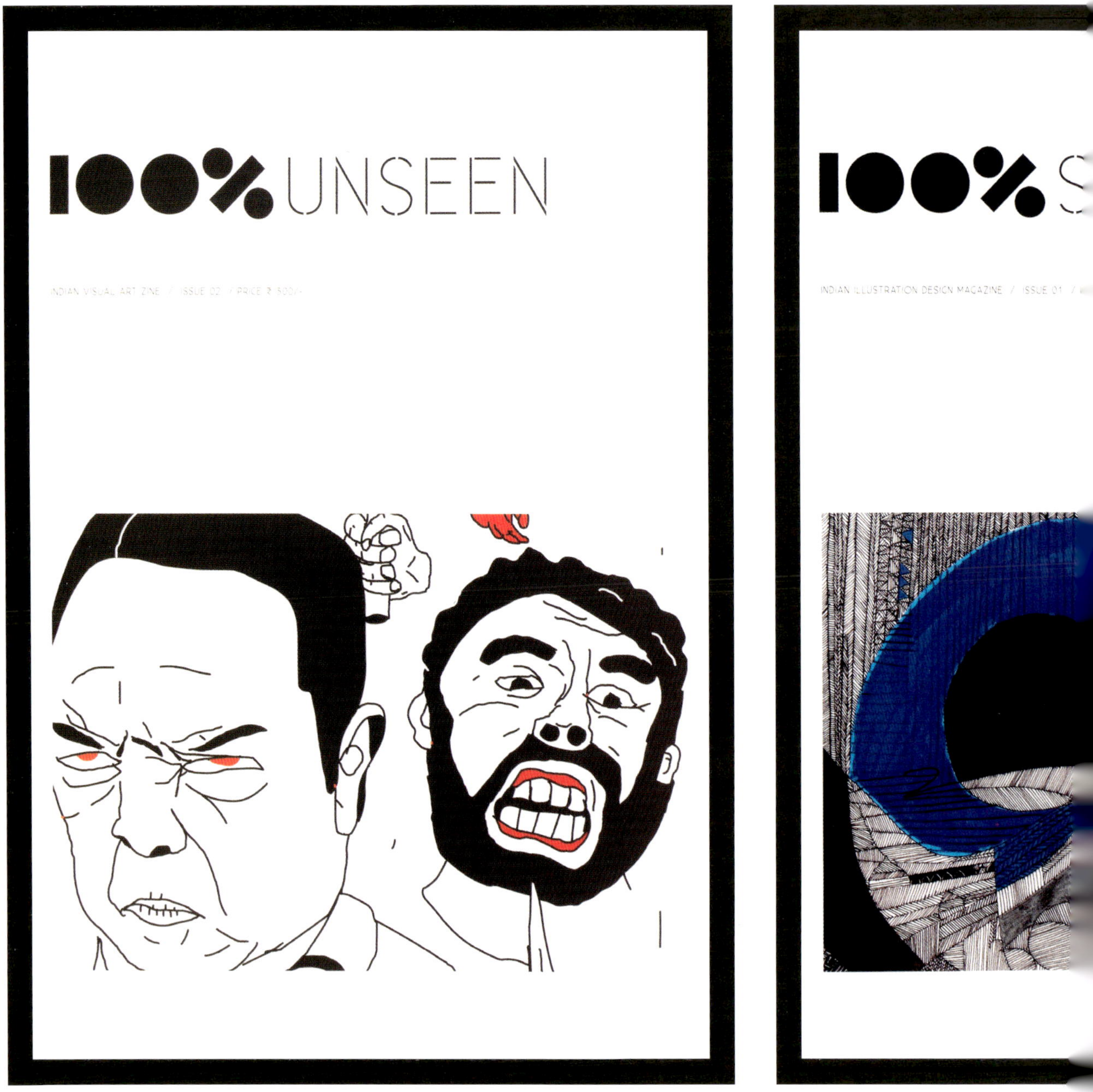

IOO% UNSEEN

INDIAN VISUAL ART ZINE / ISSUE 02 / PRICE ₹ 500/-

100% Unseen and 100% Sound.
Designed and edited by Lokesh
Karekar and Sameer Kulavoor, 2011.
Photo courtesy
V&A Museum, London.

DUND

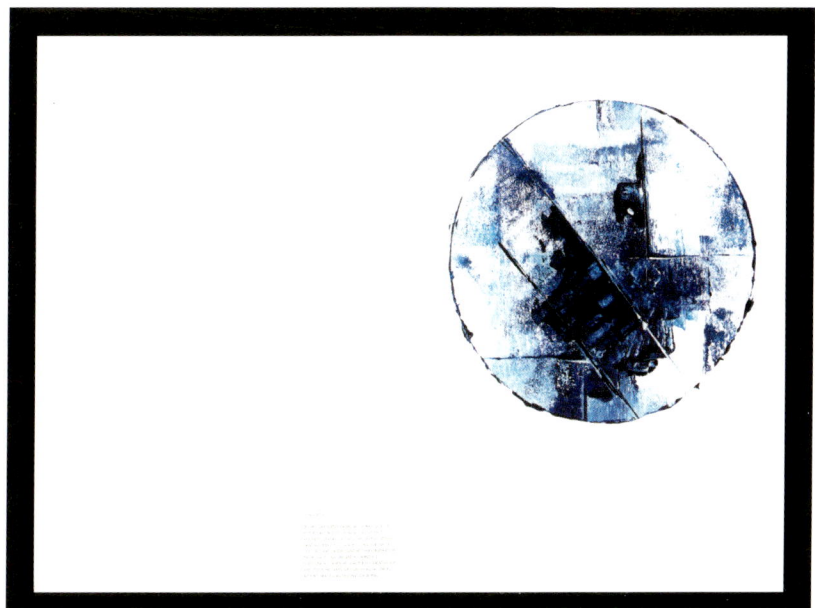

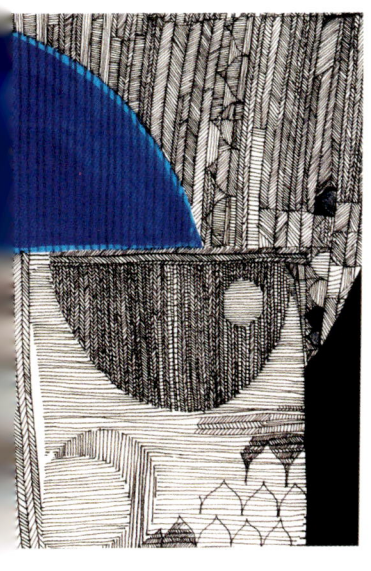

100% Sound.
Inside page with artwork
by Kunal Belo.
Designed and edited by
Lokesh Karekar and
Sameer Kulavoor, 2011.
Photo courtesy
V&A Museum, London.

of the mono-rail map. The city is a great source of inspiration in many forms, including its vernacular graphics. Taxi art, street signs, shops, film hoardings, and their method of representation, technique and aesthetic are important to many graphic designers because they convey history and meaning, both of the city and of the nation. Traditional graphics are therefore often referenced and utilized in their work because they symbolize an Indian identity.

Zines are a primary means for the followers of the 'cult of design' to enjoy and appreciate contemporary graphics. Zines are self-financed, independent and with a limited print run. They have a quality of maverick originality about them; non-conformist and experimental they offer the designer a far greater means of self-expression than client-based commissions. Locopopo and Bombay Duck Graphics have jointly produced *100%*, the first zine dedicated to the art of illustration. Only in its third issue, the first launched in 2011, each one focuses on a single topic, such as *100%* Sound or *100%* Unseen and so on. Through its scale, typography, typeface, and tactility it reflects a simple, clean, and uncluttered aesthetic that gives space to the illustrators. The size is A3, the larger-scale distinguishing it from other zines and enabling one double spread per illustrator with a full image on one and text label concentrated in the bottom right

123

Zeroxwallah.
Illustrated and designed by Sameer
Kulavoor of Bombay Duck Design, 2010.
Photo courtesy Sameer Kulavoor.

hand corner of the other. The effectiveness of the covers lies in their simplicity, the boldness of the title and its typeface with one dynamic illustration. Inside, the breath of illustration types ranging from hand-drawn and compute-aided to photography and printmaking conveys their communicative power. These zines are limited-edition collector's items, treasured for their presentation of Indian content, occasionally interspersed with global content, in a clean contemporary style with high production values.

Zeroxwallah is another which falls into this collector's category. Created by Bombay Duck Designs, it pays homage to the photo-copy shop and the photocopying district in Fort, Mumbai. Recording the multi-sensory experience familiar to many, the process is described poetically on his website as 'the fluttering of paper, the everyday counting of endless sheets contributing to the reverberating lingo, the swift movement of light through the machine...' Authenticity and replication of experience are embedded in the zine through its utilization of photocopies. The materiality of the xerox, its A4 scale, its grey finishing, all become integral to the representation of the imagery within. The zine is a detailed observation of the nuances of the photocopying experience, starting with the common misspelling of xerox and the yellow and black covers which mimic the distinctive shop signage. Inside, there is a montage reconstruction of the photocopying locality, a screen-print of a packet of toner, quirky hand-drawn illustrations, sign boards with relevant terminology, a step-by-step illustrated guide to the act of photocopying and much more. Kulavoor's surveillance of the city continues in the zine *Blued* which refers to *blue tarp* or *taad-patri*, the tarpaulin plastic sheeting utilized in a variety of functions across the city streets. These zines, enable the graphic designer to develop their own language which is vital to the evolution of the practice of graphic design and the development of a unique style. They are sold in boutiques such as Filter in the Kalaghoda district of Mumbai, where according to Kulavoor, they make a 'conscious, intelligent decision to exclude any kind of fake Indian-ness from their display.'[25] The examples explored here reflect the desire of these designers to place themselves as creative, innovative individuals, acutely attuned to India but very much part of the global landscape. Their work documents a slice of local life, in a moment in time, but it does not necessarily aim to define an Indian identity.

Living

The PARK Magazine

02

MAY - JULY 2008

Magazine Culture

Magazines have a greater formality about them; they are more structured and have some commercial constraints. The three under consideration here are case studies in approaches to graphic design. Two of them, *Living* (The Park Magazine*)* and *Motherland*, are diametrically opposed in their aesthetic, their content, and their targeted audience, but they share a wish to marry the sophistication of global production with a contemporary Indian sensibility and in doing so they encourage the appreciation of graphic design and its ability to visually enhance and facilitate communication. The third, *Seminar* magazine, is alone in its graphic treatment, in that each cover is exclusively typographic. It offers a point of contrast, conveying through its graphic treatment a sense of timelessness rather than a sign of the times.

Living magazine, launched in 2008, reflects that search for an Indian graphic style, one that is linked to India's traditions. It was designed specifically for Park hotels in key commercial cities such as Bengaluru, Delhi, Kolkata, and Hyderabad. Conceived and designed by Tania Khosla of TSK Designs, the magazine expresses the ethos of the hotels, one which places contemporary design and an Indian aesthetic as central to its boutique spaces. It is distributed to their clients, functioning as a marketing tool for the hotel facilities and as a guide to local and national creative cultures. Each issue has a broad theme and includes short articles that are lifestyle and design led and which dip into history, geography, art, craft, culture, and people.

The magazines are an illustration of an Indian aesthetic that rejoices in pattern and colour and refuses to be drawn into minimalism to be perceived as contemporary. The graphic style is impactful because of its vibrancy, which it borrows from popular and local cultures. There is minimal text on the covers, with the masthead containing only the title, while the issue number and date are integrated elsewhere. The cover image is always layered using a base photograph overlaid with a bold single-colour pattern on top. A striking example is the *Future Thought* issue, focusing on sustainability, where a photograph of piles of rubbish is overlaid with a pictogram in bright blue of a figure seated with a spinning wheel, juxtaposing the wastefulness of a modern consumerist society with indigenous traditions of resourcefulness. In addition, the first four issues are visually linked through the concept of the spiral as contained

Facing page:
Living, the Park Hotel Magazine. Designed by TSK Design, 2008-9. Photo courtesy TSK Design.

127

in the circular motion of a series of figures in yoga positions (issue 1), a spinning wheel (issue 2), a spiral of red rays shining across the face of an Indian calendar girl (issue 3), and the spiral of a pupil within a human eye (issue 4). This range of imagery, the brash juxtaposition of pattern and colour achieved with the layering technique, is the main device for contemporizing the look of the magazine. This is a very clear example of how digital technology has enabled great flexibility of technique. It is interesting to note that the fifth and sixth issues of *Living* have seen a shift in aesthetic, moving away from the multiple shocking colour palettes to using only black and red as the overlaying colours, signifying a move into a more sophisticated representation of Indian identity and its ever-changing nature.

By way of contrast and created for a different audience, *Motherland* was launched in 2010 and aimed to fill a gap in the market for a magazine that documented India's disparate and vast culture in an original and insightful manner through detailed essays that were tied together with strong graphic design. With issues entitled *Prisons, Freedom* or *Performance*, they explore India's subcultures and non-conventional themes that can be national and local in scope. The essays delve below the surface offering more than the simple sound-bites of other magazines and are coupled with striking visuals and photo essays that showcase new talent. Published by the creative agency Weiden and Kennedy (W+K), which was set up in Delhi in 2007 under the direction of V. Sunil and Mohit Jayal, the magazine reflects the ethos of an agency known for being more edgy and responsive to the younger creative public. Their reputation has been built on innovative strategies as illustrated in their work for low-cost airline, IndiGo, and through less commercial enterprises such as their in-house gallery where they showcase small-scale specialist art and design exhibitions, the aim being to take better design to a broader audience.

According to V. Sunil, 'Indian culture' has always been packaged badly with little application of design, which tends to devalue the content.[26] In their press release their approach to branding 'rejects the usual clichés of "aspirational" pseudo-western imagery and defensive in your face ethnicity, W+K's work reflects an India that is finally comfortable in its own skin. Campaigns combine regional flair, values and tastes with global aesthetics and popular culture'.[27] *Motherland* embodies this statement in its graphic design. The magazine is between an A4 and A5 size with

129

Motherland
₹100

Manipur's vigilantes
Guwahati's food heroes
Shillong: (heritage)
rock capital?
Tourism's front line:
travel outfits and peace building
Bright young things: Nagaland's
first generation entrepreneurs
Football to unite groups in conflict
The Nagaland café churning
out revolutionary ideas
Spoken word: why a culture of orality is a
raison d'être for writers in the Northeast
Manipur's icon: Irom Sharmila
photographed by Gauri Gill
And more...

ISSN 0976-8319   INR ₹100
USD $6
EUR €8
UK £5
JPY ¥1,000

Motherland
₹100

Ghost Stories

ISBN 978-81-924054-0-7   INR ₹100
EUR €7.5
AED 25

Motherland
₹100

Prisons

ISSN 0976-8319   INR ₹100
EUR €7.5

Motherland
₹100

Wedding bands:
the end of an era?
The tattooed folk of Chhattisgarh
Music festivals come of age
India's serial impersonators
The Delhi farmhouse - a requisite
playground
Kashmir's wedding banquet wizzes
Flower power (and other political
party symbols)
The Calcutta "purtee"
The political party winning
hearts and votes
And more...

ISSN 0976-8319   INR ₹100
USD $6
EUR €8
UK £5
JPY ¥1,000

a cover that is always simple, bold and occasionally provocative. The masthead consists of the title in a script typeface which conveys a tone of elegance and refinement. An emphatic full-stop at the end of the title contains a globe with a map of India, a visual symbol of *Motherland*. A simple pattern of diamonds, which separates the masthead from the main body of the cover, is evidence of the attention to detail throughout the magazine. While earlier issues have multiple coverlines informing the reader of the main stories, more recent ones demonstrate a change in design strategy which enhances its visual impact. The later covers are reduced exclusively to title, image and theme which take the form of one word in the centre of the page in a bold confident typeface. Thus, the image, colour, positioning and typeface are composed to project a tone and message of non-conformity, creativity and authority. After two years and eight issues, V. Sunil is still experimenting with the format to appeal to a larger target audience of creative young people and consequently to generate a greater appreciation of contemporary design. The smaller size has been perceived as being too academic and exclusive, therefore the April 2013 issue was significantly larger in size to enable it to standout on the magazine stands, thus making it more accessible.

Inside, the style is contemporary, but not minimal. Quirky detailing such as the decorative font used for the page numbering, the scallop patterns on the bottom edges of the page, the occasional ornate framing of the text and images all add subtle points of interest and draw the viewer's attention across the page. The source of inspiration for these elements are unusual, refreshing, and reflective of an intelligent non-clichéd referencing of heritage. They borrow from Indian currency notes; a quick glance at a range of notes shows the clever way in which their fine and subtle design elements have been re-purposed within the magazine. It is a refreshing and intelligent means of contemporizing an aesthetic based on heritage. These elements are not a 'defensive in your face ethnicity', rather they allude to the ornamentation and decorative patterning that is historically associated with Indian design and for which it was much prized in Europe in the mid-19th century. At the Great Exhibition of 1851 in London, it was celebrated for the 'rich invention shown in patterns, in which the beauty, distinctness, and variety of forms, and the harmonious blending of severe colours, called forth the admiration of all true judges of art, what a lesson such designs afford to manufacturers, even in those nations of Europe which have made the greatest progress in Industry.'[28] This also addresses broader debates about the relevance

Facing page:
(Clockwise from top left)
Motherland magazine, front cover.
Issue 4, 2011.
Issue 7, 2012.
Issue 3, 2011.
Issue 6, 2012.
Photo courtesy Motherland.

Following pages:
Left above: 'Paris, Milan, Dimapur' in *Motherland*, issue 4, 2011.
Text and page design by Motherland.
Photo courtesy Tenzing Dakpa.

Left below: 'The Wonder Tree' in *Motherland*, issue 5, 2011.
Text and page design by Motherland.
Photo courtesy Motherland.

Right above: 'Vedic Astrology' in *Motherland*, issue 2, 2010.
Text and page design by Motherland.
Photo courtesy Motherland.

Right below: 'Respect. OK?' in *Motherland*, issue 2, 2010.
Text and page design by Motherland.
Photo courtesy Motherland.

VILINA ACHUMI, 22, Bachelor of Commerce graduate

"BECAUSE OF OUR ANTI-INDIAN SENTIMENT THEIR CLOTHES COULD NOT BE ACCEPTED," SAYS YANGER WHO RECALLS WEARING BELL-BOTTOMS IN THE 1970s.

NGAOPUNI RADO, 20, high school graduate

THE WONDER TREE

Not all trees were born equal, and the coconut tree is a cut above the rest; it's not just a cash crop, but one of nature's marvels, one that can literally provide a person with anything they may need to survive. In the southern Indian state of Kerala, appropriately named after the coconut tree (kera, coconut tree; alam, land), of which it is abundant in, this tree has assumed iconic status. Here, every last bit of a coconut palm is put to multifarious uses: coconut water, inebriating toddy, oil for food, hair and skin; coir (an English word derived from its Malayalam equivalent) for mats and rope; leaves for roofing; timber for homes; charcoal, and more. There seems to be little limit to what an enterprising culture can do with this palm, and while these practices may not go as far back as the tree itself (around at least 37 million years), they're a mark of a way of life that has been eco-friendly much before that was even a word in the dictionary.

The toddy is to Kerala what Guinness is to Ireland; it's a staple at local roadside bars or toddy shops. Toddy is made from palm sap, which starts fermenting from the time it's extracted to become an alcoholic brew within just a few hours time.

VEDIC ASTROLOGY:
THE FIVE MOST ASKED QUESTIONS

TEXT
ANNALISA
MERELLI

Childbirth, relationships, marriage, business and death – these are the five most asked topics by clients of Vedic astrologers, says Dhananjay Sharma of soothsayers-india. com. While there is no changing your destiny, says another astrologer Dr Prem Kumar Sharma, visiting an astrologer can direct you towards making the best decisions according to what the stars have in store for you.

CHILDBIRTH.

With the increasing number of caesarean sections, destiny as it were, becomes somewhat murkier. According to Vedic astrology, the place, day and hour of birth are fundamental in determining the fate of an individual. But when the time of birth is no longer Mother Nature's call, but that of expecting parents, fixing a day for a c-section means that the onus of that child's fate lies with the parents.

Luckily, Vedic astrologers can be versatile: once the doctor has indicated the range of days on which the c-section has to happen, the astrologer works out astrological charts that correspond to the different days and times suggested, enabling parents to chose between a few options for their child's destiny.

RELATIONSHIPS AND MARRIAGE.

Dhananjay Sharma says that while Western clients are more concerned about relationship problems, Indians tend to focus on marriage: will they marry and when? Dr Prem Kumar Sharma says over his 35 year career, he has issued countless couples with pre-marital advice, using astrological charts to determine whether or not their match was quite literally, made in heaven. An astrologer can also help choose the day of the wedding. Some auspicious dates are commonly known (May 16, 2010 was a favourite this year and between Mumbai and Delhi, 75,000 weddings took place), but even then, it is better to consult the family astrologer to make sure the date is compatible with a couple's charts.

BUSINESS

One may think that astrology is a ladies' affair, but men visit soothsayers just as often and largely to seek advice on how to run a business better. Dr Prem Kumar Sharma says business affairs may require the constant assistance of an astrologer. While most clients visit their soothsayer from once a month to twice a year, a businessman in the middle of a difficult transaction might see his astrologer every week to seek his guidance.

An astrologer is believed to be able to help alter the destiny of a business before it has even started. Did you know that choosing a company name was simply a matter of creativity and marketing skills? Well, it isn't that simple. A company name can have many implications, and once a name is decided upon, an astrologer can help alter the letter count, which can impact a business.

That is, explains Dhananjay Sharma, the reason behind all the unusual spellings of Indian brands: the extra vowels, or k in lieu of c, or repeated consonants may be chosen to improve the destiny of the business, and not just to sound unique.

DEATH

Astrologers are very adamant that there is nothing to be done about changing one's destiny. Yet this doesn't seem to stop people from asking soothsayers about their own death. We can't help wondering that if indeed the predicted date and time of death was inaccurate, and a client happened to outlive his astrological self, would there actually be cause for complaint!

The formidable and intellectually appealing exercise of demystifying the success of a superstar is, in reality, fraught with futility – as if trying to explain exactly why the traditionally bland palates of the British were tickled by sizzling platefuls of Tandoori Chicken.

So why is a star a star? The reason is usually a mystical and propitious convergence of need, taste, branding and marketing, choice of films and roles, word of mouth, and a few hundred other obscure factors. Take Amitabh Bachchan, Bollywood's first superstar in the masala hero mould. For years, we've been supping on the urban legend that Bachchan's personification of the angry young man spoke loud and clear to a nation disillusioned by a callous and corrupt establishment, and that's why he became a superstar. But how does the righteous clown of *Amar Akbar Anthony* fit into this paradigm? Or the brooding romantic of *Kabhi Kabhie*? Or the timid English professor of *Chupke Chupke*? Or the hedonistic gangster (and hearty simpleton) of *Don*? Can we pinpoint with certainty which facets of the actor appealed most to the audience of the 1970s that birthed this superstar?

All we can say is that the actor appealed to audiences and that's the conclusion too, even before beginning the admittedly theoretical task of unravelling the appeal of Rajinikanth – the superstar from Tamil Nadu whose reign has far outstripped that of Bachchan's. Despite the fact that Tamil language films typically receive little attention outside the state, at least in comparison to the nationwide noise Bollywood productions make. And if adulation is taken into account, Rajinikanth is far and away the bigger superstar. Where Bachchan's fans demonstrate their loyalty by simply queuing up at the box office for his latest release, Rajinikanth's legions of admirers from fan clubs gather around giant cut-outs of the star, like devotees before a god. They bathe their idol with litres of milk, and firecrackers are set off in theatres to celebrate the arrival of their god's latest avatar.

What explains his longevity? Or the hysteria he still whips up? And more curiously, what explains the national media's inquisition into the Rajini phenomenon each time he has a film ready for release? The latter is the most interesting development in the far-reaching and fabulous career of the former bus conductor known as Shivaji Rao Gaekwad. That Rajinikanth has long been the cynosure of Tamil eyes needs no recounting – a star of supreme stature in the Tamil-speaking pockets of the universe. But now, his films are dubbed in Hindi and national publications are deluged with editorials trying to make sense of the Rajini phenomenon, if only to convince themselves that the colonisation of a national mind space by a southern star cannot occur without a semblance of logical reason.

And as is so often the case when attempting to explain the inexplicable, it's the clichés that come to the fore – the twirling of the sunglasses, the flipping of the cigarette, the gesticulations enhanced by whiplash sound effects. And the outlandishly exaggerated action sequences rivalled only by the outlandishly exaggerated punch dialogues, like the one from *Sivaji (The Boss)* where he tells a villain, who jeers that he's all alone and outnumbered, that only a swine needs the comfort of numbers, not lions like him. (*Kanna, panningo dhaan kootama varum. Singam single-aa dhaan varum.*)

These clichés are probably the primary appeal of Rajinikanth to a modern-day northern viewer only acquainted with the actor's more recent films, made fashionable by media hype To them, he is a cartoon character of flesh and blood, a fount of thigh-slapping humour so bad it's good. The Rajinikanth who made a mild splash as a leading man in the Hindi cinema of the 1980s lies forgotten. He is now an outré embodiment of the worst (and therefore most entertaining) excesses of Bollywood before it came to be known as Bollywood, namely the "illogical" masala movies of the 1970s. And his films are viewed – with ironic and amused detachment and perhaps even mild condescension – as the *desi* equivalent of campy grindhouse flicks.

Audiences from Tamil Nadu, however, have a more complex history with the star, which harks back not just to the actor's introduction in the

Rajinikanth's legions of admirers from fan clubs gather around giant cut-outs of the star, like devotees before a god.

That Rajinikanth has long been the cynosure of Tamil eyes needs no recounting – a star of supreme stature in the Tamil-speaking pockets of the universe.

seminar

636 august 2012 www.india-seminar.com

of ornamentation in contemporary graphic design. The work of Denise Gonzales Crisp and Daniel van der Velden argues that ornament in graphic design can be empathetic, provide escape, be playful, enable multiple narratives, embed history and generally allow for a greater expression in visual vocabulary than the modernist principles of clean lines and minimalism.[29] Therefore, in combining local stories and local design elements within broader global production values and aesthetics, *Motherland* is an appropriate representation of the times, a symbol of the local-global culture of a young creative India. In the words of one reader, Brijesh Patel, 'It is for me a merger of *Monocle, Intelligent Life* and *New Yorker*, blended into one very Indian but also very global magazine from a global country. I look forward to discovering more of this India...'[30]

Seminar magazine offers a lesson in graphic timelessness rather than concerning itself with representing identity. This may be a reflection of the time of its founding, in 1959, which suggests and re-enforces the idea that anxiety or need to convey a sense of identity in design has developed with post-liberalization and as a response to the globalizing environment. *Seminar* magazine's typographic covers perfectly suit the text-rich, intellectual content. It was set up my Raj and Romesh Thapar as an experimental exercise that 'became the hallowed "Adda" – a bridge between the students, academicians, intellectuals, artists, politicians, bureaucrats, radicals, change-agents, eccentrics, socialites, and attention-grabbers – nurturing their discourse, chiselling their ideologies, and giving them a voice'.[31] Having enlisted renowned academics and journalists as contributors, it is a reputed journal tackling issues of social and economic relevance. The typographic covers initially designed by Dilip Chowdhury Associates were always an indication of an alternative independent magazine.

Since the 1990s most of the covers have been designed by Akila Seshasayee of Sesh Design.[32] They are bold, dramatic and often stark, never using more than three colours and often only two. The covers examined here are examples of how important subjects of the post-liberalization period have been represented typographically. For each issue, the masthead remains the same, and additional information such as the date, issue number, and website address are creatively integrated into the typographic treatment. The covers range from those that are a simple and instant visualization of the concept to those that make the viewer stop and consider the meaning. Typographic creativity involves

135

the imagining of metaphoric type, negotiating the visual relationships of scale and space, positive form and void, rhythm and balance to convey meaning through composition, juxtaposition, and manipulation.

Simple and instant covers include that for *Globalization* (July 2001), where the uncertainties and ambiguities of its impact on India are conveyed through the simple splitting and shifting of the letter G. Similarly, the population issue entitled *Beyond Numbers* (May 2002) uses colour differentiation and the clever insertion of multiples of the figure 0 to create impact. Other covers are more complex, such as *Democratising Knowledge* (August 2011). This issue focused on changes to the higher education system, making it more accessible, inclusive, and multidirectional. To convey this, Akila employed the arrow as a dominant motif, using the counterforms of the letters M, A, K, and W to form arrows which point in both directions. These key letters were also enlarged and repeated in the centre like an acronym.[33] Although Akila recognized the potential difficulty of readers in deciphering the design, the editors felt that it was important in some cases for readers to 'pause and really look'.[34] Two issues which explore traditions and their modern relevance are *Between Cultures* (July 2007), which conveys the clash of past and present in the city of Lucknow by overlaying different fonts, and *The Enduring Epic* (April 2010), a study of the *Mahabharata* in present times. The design for this was by Divya Kukreti of Sesh Studios and is 'a representation of the *chakravyuha*, the disc-like military formation used in the famous battle of Kurukshetra which is recounted in the poem. Here, the designer has created the disc from multiple repetitions of the title, which, seen as an abstract, can allude to tree rings denoting age but also suggests an echo, conveying the oral nature of the poem'.[35] Urban expansion also demands attention in two issues, one which focuses on *Urban Transformation* (May 2012) and the other on the *Street Scape* (August 2012). The former makes use of street maps and the latter reflects the chaos of the new and rapid urban growth in which the letterforms mimick buildings, roads, metro systems, and built structures overshadow people thus conveying a sense of the urban-jungle. In these post-liberalization issues, the typographic cover continues to make an impact, demonstrating the flexibility of graphic design as a tool for the imparting of meaning.

Left to right and then top to bottom:
Seminar Magazine, front cover.
The Democratising of Knowledge, Issue no. 624, 2011.
Urban Transformations, Issue no. 635, 2012.
Globalisation, Issue no. 503, 2001.
Between Cultures, Issue no. 575, 2007.
Beyond Numbers, Issue no. 511, 2002.
Designed by Akila Seshasayee.
Image courtesy Akila Seshasayee.

The Enduring Epic, Issue no. 608, 2010.
Designed by Divya Kukreti.
Image courtesy Akila Seshasayee.

137

As a communication design practice, how do you build narratives for spaces?

Our approach from the start has been to understand what is it that a client wants to communicate, to see the story that he has to tell, share in the excitement of that story and look at ways to tell the story in a more interesting manner. Building narratives for spaces is part of the larger goal that the client shares and, in fact, all our space design projects have been supported by interventions in the print, the digital and web media.

We usually look for goals that sometimes go beyond the client's immediate brief. In many cases, our space designs have been instrumental in repositioning the organisation and in it being perceived in a new light. In the case of a paint manufacturer, an exhibition for colour forecast meant it being viewed as a proactive visionary. In the case of an institute of biological sciences, an exhibition on the early botanical knowledge of sixteenth century India gave it a certain visibility at both the national and international level as an institute whose goals were beyond research objectives.

So whether we are conceiving formal corporate messaging for a reception area, or an informal, fun and stimulating café as a break out space for a corporate environment – we look into the experience we want the user to have. Both these complementary treatments are thought out deliberately as different facets of the larger brand personality of the same organisation.

We usually look for goals that sometimes go beyond the client's immediate brief.

The *Collector Memory* installation, part of the *ROAR* exhibition, invited contributions from people of Mumbai, witness to the deluge of 2005.

It's only natural for an artist or artisan to get agitated when someone from outside starts messing around with their craft —some may feel that the way they have learnt is the only way. Raghunath's temperament was different. Anytime we proposed anything unusual or difficult, he would say "yes, yes, let us try this" and would want to jump right into it. So we really got along! We would go and live there —stay with him, eat with the family, and go to the printing table and print ourselves. In that process, we both figured out various things that we could play with.

Traditional block printers were losing out to the fact that screen printing could actually create 'perfectly' printed fabric faster and cheaper. Raghunath understood that. So we started to explore what we could do with block printing that we could not with screen printing. With blocks, you could take one element and repeat it in many ways—you could twist it, you could space it out and two different things. The immense variety in play we were creating on the T-shirts could not be replicated via screen printing except at a huge cost. We kept experimenting and the T-shirts came out really good.

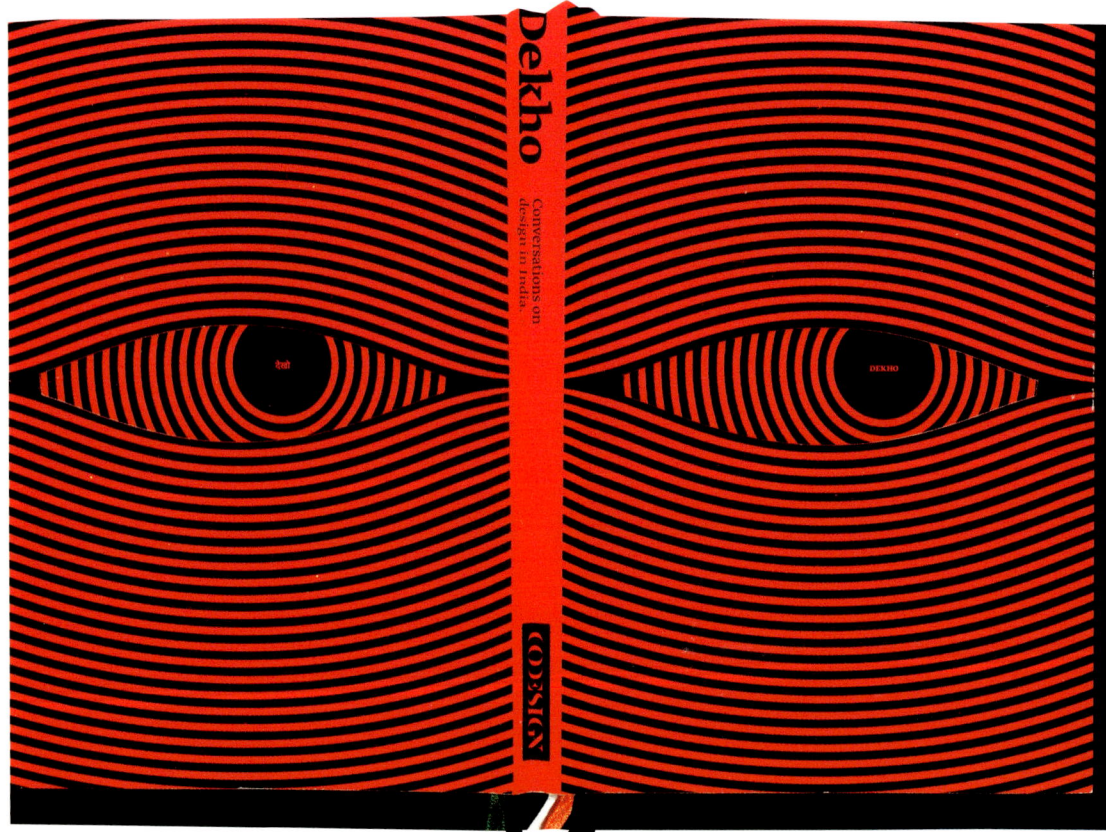

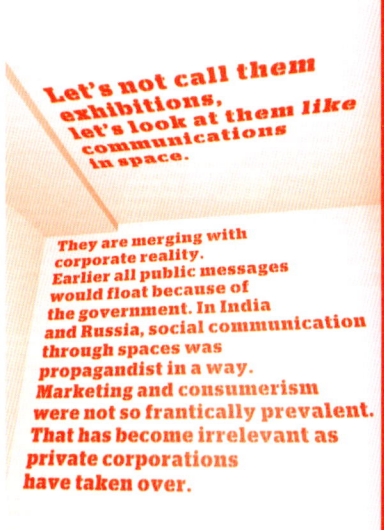

Our approach
to design
is
craft.

Let's not call them exhibitions, let's look at them like communications in space.

They are merging with corporate reality. Earlier all public messages would float because of the government. In India and Russia, social communication through spaces was propagandist in a way. Marketing and consumerism were not so frantically prevalent. That has become irrelevant as private corporations have taken over.

Exhibitions have lost meaning, but now they're finding their feet in new media, experimenting with experiences that are more immersive with greater impact. A heightened sense of reality has taken over us. The screen can no longer hold our attention; it is a less memorable experience because of the exposure you have to it.

In this context, creating a personality in a space is gaining importance.

194_Amar In The Making

195

Book Design

Book design offers a more permanent means of expressing graphic creativity. The examples offered here are disparate in nature; they convey very different yet equally relevant approaches to graphic design in this field. *Dekho* is an anthology of conversations about approaches to designing for India. Codesign, a brand and communication design practice, are responsible for gathering the information, editing, and designing the book. Rajesh Dahiya, who heads the team behind its production, is keen to shift perceptions of graphic design away from over-exposed versions of Indian-ness, particularly those which reference popular culture and present instead a multiplicity of ideas derived from a diverse set of influences, all of which are context-led. This book is a very personal journey of discovery for the team; it is self-published and engages with the work of people whom are well-known to them; each conversation is therefore invested with an 'aesthetic that it deserves', resulting in a different graphic style to suit the context of the individual stories.[36] Dahiya's respect for Stefan Sagmeister and Wolfgang Weingart, internationally renowned graphic designers, is shown through their inclusion in the book. Their influence on the book design is apparent in

139

the rebellious and challenging nature of the typography: Not confined to a clear and uniform demarcation of text from image throughout, there is the conceptualization of each story into an original graphic landscape which builds in a deliberate complexity that requires a slow and determined unwrapping of information. As noted in the introduction: 'The book is designed not just to be read from start to finish, but with multiple layers of image and text, it is meant to be experienced anew, with each new story and each new page.'[37]

For an essay entitled 'Of the head, hand and heart, capturing the story of People Tree', which is about the creation of sustainable livelihoods for crafts people, textile dyers and printers in Jaipur, the graphic treatment evokes coloured dyes dissolving in water. The graphic response to a story on the typesetting of Indian languages based on the sound of the spoken word is to juxtapose visual representations of sound, speech, and script. *Kerning Space*, a graphic term for the space between letter forms, is the title given to a conversation about spatial design. Here the graphic treatment reflects the way in which the design studio under consideration explores beyond the brief to create innovative solutions for exhibition design. The graphic visualization of phrases such as 'Beyond the box' (pages 139-140) and 'As in most engaging communication, it is finally not just what is said, but how it is said' (pages 142-3) is not executed in a manner which offers an instantaneous reading; instead, there is a requirement that the reader have the curiosity and interest to work it out. They are meant to instil an element of playfulness into the proceedings, a quality which the studio instils into its spatial installations. Codesign has employed a variety of features, fonts, symbols, illustrations, and visual metaphors which, depending on the sensibility of the reader, can either stimulate or distract them from the information.

A publisher which has been at the forefront of new approaches to book design, illustration and for its support of diverse and non-mainstream projects that take inspiration from folk art, popular culture and the global publishing scene is Tara Books. *In the Land of Punctuation* by Christian Morgenstern was released in 2009 and enabled Rathna Ramanathan to use typography as illustration. Taking a modernist approach and executed in black, white, and red, punctuation marks are envisioned as characters able to express meaning and emotion through scale, rhythm, colour, and placement.[38] Tara Books are renowned for

Facing page:
In the Land of Punctuation. Written by Christian Morgenstern. Illustrated and designed by Rathna Ramanathan. Copyright Tara Books 2009. Photo courtesy V&A Museum, London.

140

The semicolons' mournful racket
is drowned out by surrounding brackets

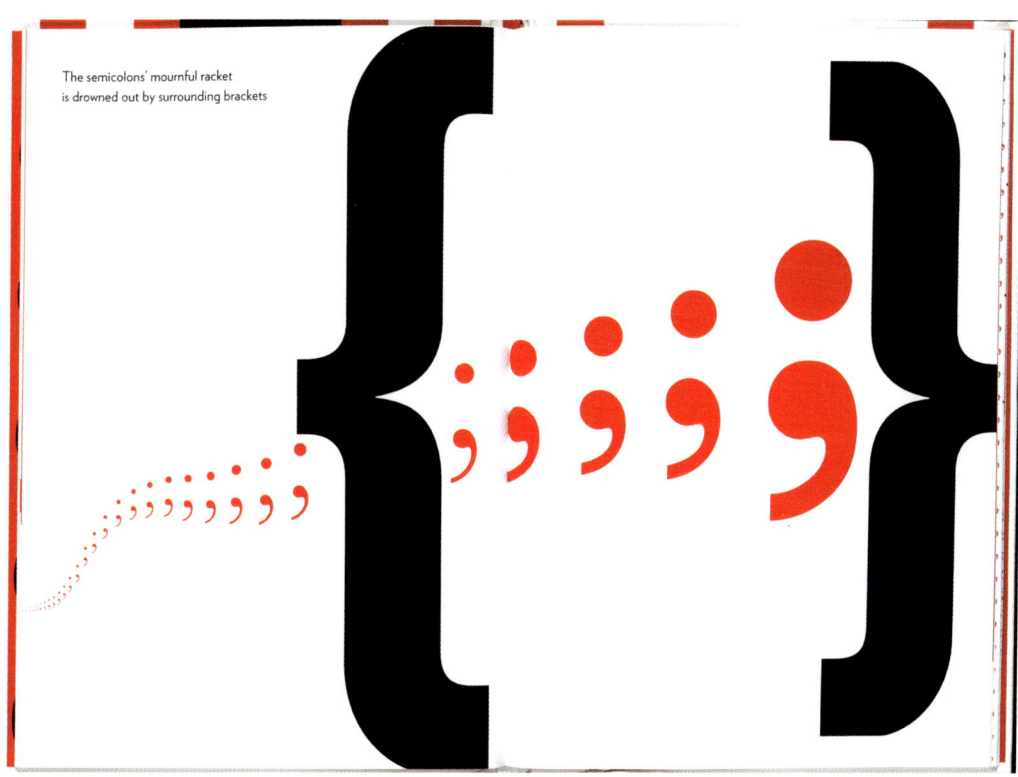

And cut across the commas necks
so that the beheaded wrecks

(the dashes delight in gore)
as semi-colons hit the floor.

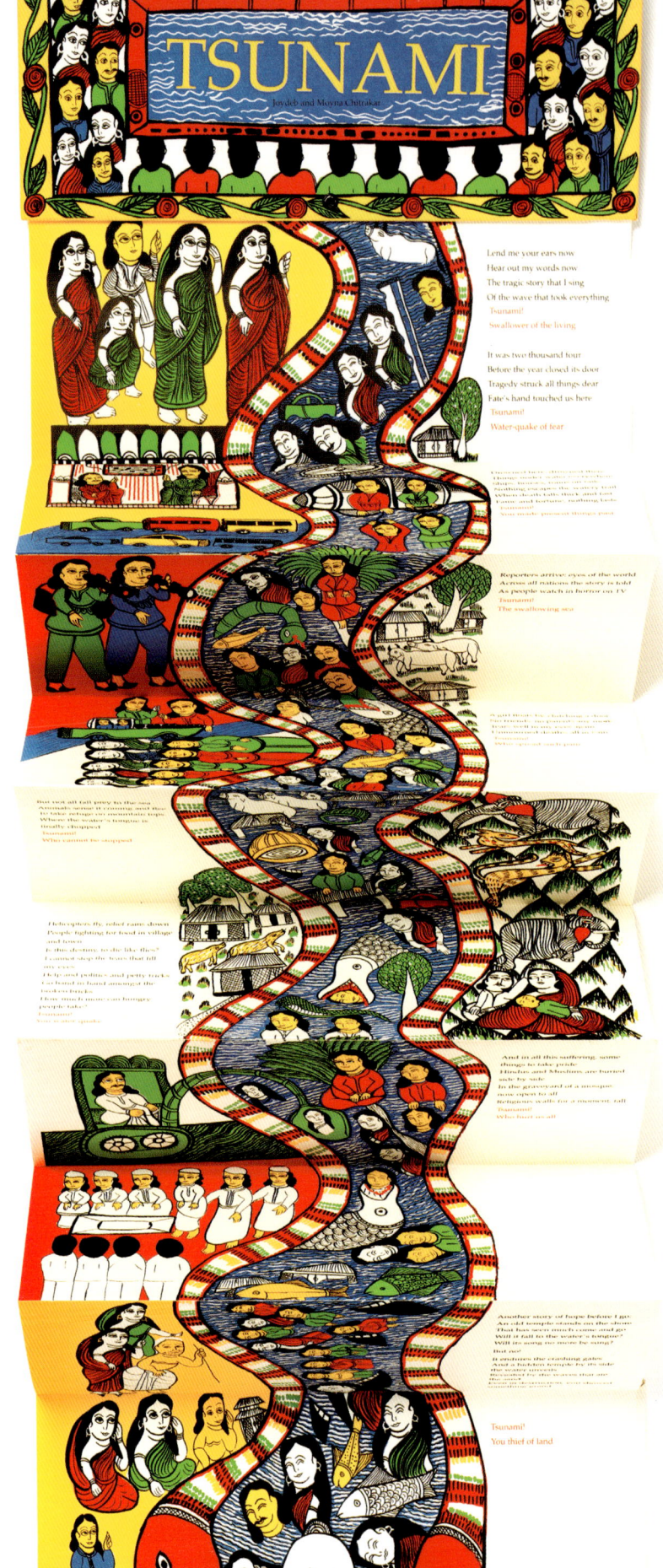

Tsunami.
Illustrated by Joydeb
and Moyna Chitrakar.
Designed by Rathna
Ramanathan.
Copyright Tara Books 2009.
Photo courtesy
V&A Museum, London.

Facing page:
Sita's Ramayana.
Illustrated by Moyna Chitrakar.
Written by Samhita Arni.
Designed by
Jonathan Yamakami.
Copyright Tara Books 2011.
Photo courtesy
V&A Museum, London.

●　●　●　INDIA Contemporary Design

their innovative promotion of folk artists and folk mediums through contemporary forms as seen in *Sita's Ramayana* by Samhita Arni and Moyna Chitrakar and *Tsunami* by Joydeb and Moyna Chitrakar, the first being a female re-telling of a classic male-focused story, and the latter a folk perspective of a contemporary incident.[39] A significant part of their process is the elevation of the status of the designer and illustrator to that of the writer, making the book an equal collaboration.[40] *Tsunami* is a hand-made book which has contemporized the oral and pictorial tradition of storytelling by the Patua community of West Bengal. The *patua* artists paint scrolls to illustrate their oral story telling. As they sing the narrative, the scroll unwinds to reveal the next episode. The Hindu epic poems the *Ramayana* and the *Mahabharata* have been recounted using this method for generations. Today, the *patua* artists cater for the tourist market in producing scrolls that convey topical news, both local and global. The re-designing of the scroll format into a book gives it a contemporary dimension whilst maintaining its function. For Gita Wolf, the founder of Tara Books, the aesthetic of the book must not override the function.[41] The use of screen-printing has maintained the look and the tactile nature of the hand-painted original. The verses of the poem, normally sung, are printed alongside the relevant images. The body of the scroll is folded and concertinaed between the front and back covers, which are not joined with a spine, thus allowing the book to be experienced as a scroll. Exposing the work of these marginalized folk artists, highlighting a traditional art form but enabling it to have a contemporary manifestation, encouraging alternative readings of texts, create a sense of social empowerment. In *Sita's Ramayana*, the designer, Jonathan Yamakami, has contemporized the traditional scroll presentation favoured by the *patua* artist by placing the illustrations into a conventional graphic novel format with the narrative moving through sequential rectangular boxes. Several devices convey the dynamism of the story: the bold, expressive illustrations, the interpretation and placement of details such as the leaping ocean or the blackness to convey sleep, the clean and efficient speech bubbles and narrative devices all impart a contemporary design aesthetic to a traditional painting style. This visual interpretation reflects the alternative nature of this contemporary reading of an ancient story.[42] Tara Books, through their regular engagement with such issues, play an important social role.

A graphic novel that offers an interesting perspective on book design is *Bhimayana: Experiences of Untouchability*, which tells the story of Bhimrao Ambedkar: a journey from poverty and extreme caste prejudice to political leader and architect of the Indian constitution. The story consists of a selection of key episodes by S. Anand and Srividya Natarajan.[43] The effectiveness of the book design is due to structural and associative typography. Structure refers to the organization of the text, and other information, while associative, reflects the ideas represented in the narrative. Storyteller, illustrators, and designers work closely together with constant revisions and adaptations to suit each other's function. An explanation of the process behind the book is incorporated within.[44] The overall impression of the novel's graphic style is intriguing, bold, expressive, and unconventional. The pages are dynamic with a sense of profuse activity; they combine image, speech, and newspaper reports to convey the power and emotive qualities of the narrative. A number of tools support and enhance ideas contained in the narrative; the most distinct aspects of associative typography include the style of illustration, the sectional devices used to separate the narrative episodes, and the development of a new typeface.

The episodes are illustrated by Durgabhai and Subhas Vyam, two artists from the Pardhan Gond tribe located in the state of Madhya Pradesh in central India. Artists (called folk/tribal) are rarely given equal status to urban art-school trained artists. Here, their creativity, and the marginalized community they represent, symbolizes the message of the narrative: a desire for equality. Stylistically, the non-realistic illustrations, highly patterned yet simple in form, are part of a sophisticated visual language that conveys the complexities of the narrative episodes. Structurally, there is no linear movement across the pages from left to right through sequential boxes as in a conventional graphic novel; instead the development of a more fluid means of sectional demarcation by the artists, and their placement on the page by the designer, has resulted in a very dynamic visual means of organizing the narrative. The demarcations consist of bands of patterning formed from thin black lines. The patterns are inspired by dignas: traditional designs applied to walls and floors in Gond homes. This tool was developed by the artists to create a loose organizational structure that allowed their characters to breathe, thereby signifying a sense of freedom from the page.[45]

An examination of two pages from the novel demonstrates these graphic tools in operation. Ambedkar's early school days are depicted on page 19. Using the open structure created through the use of the *dignas*,

145

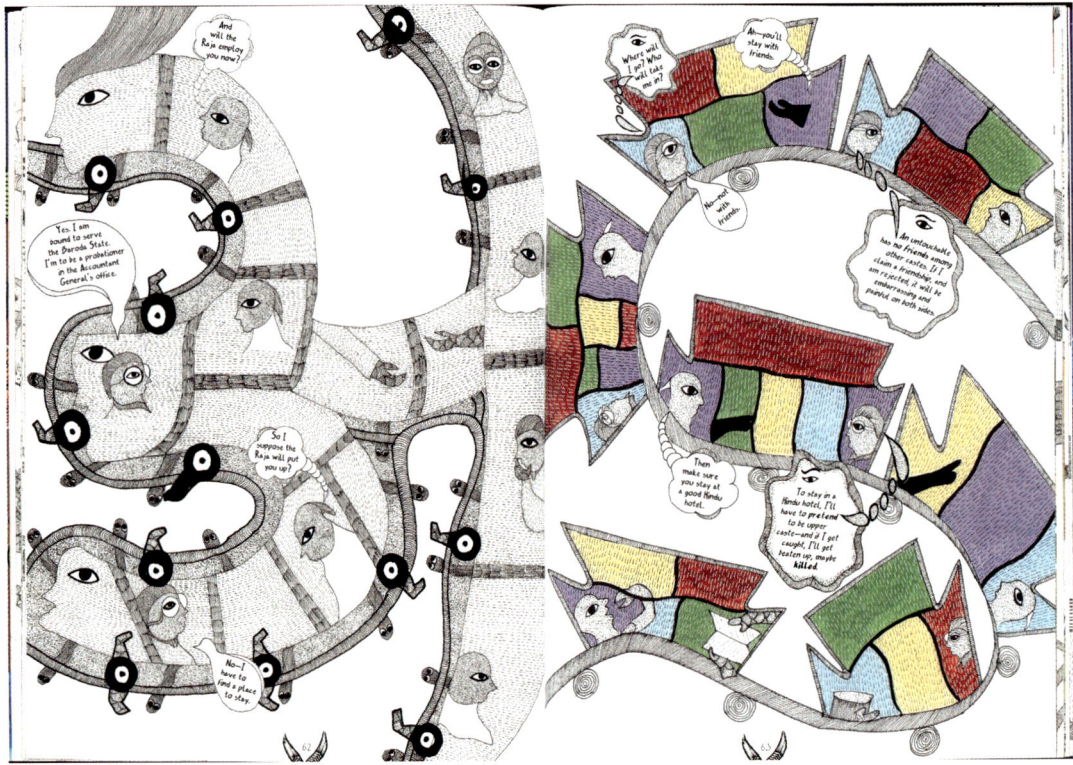

Facing page:

Bhimayana: Experiences of Untouchability, pages 19 and 63. Illustrated and designed by Durgabhai, Subhas Vyam and S. Anand, 2011. Photo courtesy V&A Museum, London.

the eye is made to wander through the page, the characters move from scene to scene in a free-flowing organic manner in keeping with the ethos of the Gond illustrative style. Hence on one page this structure is able to relate several incidents of caste prejudice in an instant. Page 63 illustrates Ambedkar's train journey from Mumbai to Baroda. The movement of the train is implied by the way it winds across the page; the compartments are an enlarged version of one of the *digna* patterns, with the colours adding a sense of dynamism to the whole. Ambedkar and his companion appear in each of the seven compartments; their conversation is conveyed through the differing thought bubbles and speech bubbles which highlight the nature of the characters. Bubbles with stinging scorpion tails represent words to be wary of; those that are bird-shaped contain innocent words and those that contain the 'mind's eye' reflect inner thoughts. The specially-designed font, entitled Bhim, simulates simple handwriting, making the speech appear informal, less alienating, and reflective of the concepts of equality and accessibility within the narrative. The artists have also incorporated symbolism within their illustrations; they envisioned Ambedkar as a fish, signifying his thirst for knowledge and action. In one of the first depictions of Bhim, his backbone takes the form of a fish, in other instances, at the suggestion of the designer, it has been used as a framing device. The fish is also the basis for another font in the book which is used for the chapter headings and the decorative feature containing the page numbers. As a whole, these elements combine to present a book that is a symbol of its message: that of equality and dynamism of the human spirit.

Typeface Design

Responding to the ascent of India on the global landscape, Peter Bilak and Satya Rajpurohit set up the Indian Type Foundry in 2009. They recognized the fundamental need to communicate better on the local and national level in relation to utilitarian functions such as street signage, forms, newspapers and so forth and are the first company to develop and distribute digital fonts, with the aim of covering all major Indian scripts.

For some graphic designers, a response to the changing urban context has been a concern over the desire to express an Indian identity within typeface design. Often their exploration is a personal journey of discovery, rather than a practical solution, offering an opportunity to better understand traditions and vernacular practices. The importance of the vernacular in any history of graphic design has to be acknowledged, particularly when it co-exists with westernized forms of graphic design; Piers Carey's study of graphic traditions from contemporary South Africa argues the same.[46] In India, hand-painted street signs, packaging and typography, with their ability to communicate with directness and immediacy and their exotic appeal, have resulted in a number of image-based books by non-Indian publishers.[47] The exceptions to this include the documentation of matchbox covers by Shahid Datawala, the academic studies of the visual culture of Calendar Art by Kajri Jain, and a selection of shorter but informative articles.[48] Typocity is a web-based documentation project that captures the typography of the city of Mumbai from street and shops signs to taxi art.[49] This interest in documenting the vernacular originates from practising graphic designers, those aware of their heritage and their role in culture-making.

Ishan Khosla Design studio has initiated Typecraft, a project that seeks to create an Indian typeface. It began with a commission to create a graphic identity for a three-year programme engaging with craft and design based in India and Australia. The project name *Sangam*, which means 'confluence', was chosen by the design team as it symbolized the programme's ethos of 'bringing together'. The graphic identity was based on a study of a variety of Indian embroidery techniques. Inspired by the motifs and shapes that constitute the visual language of *Dhebaria Rabari* embroidery, they created a digital typeface, its

149

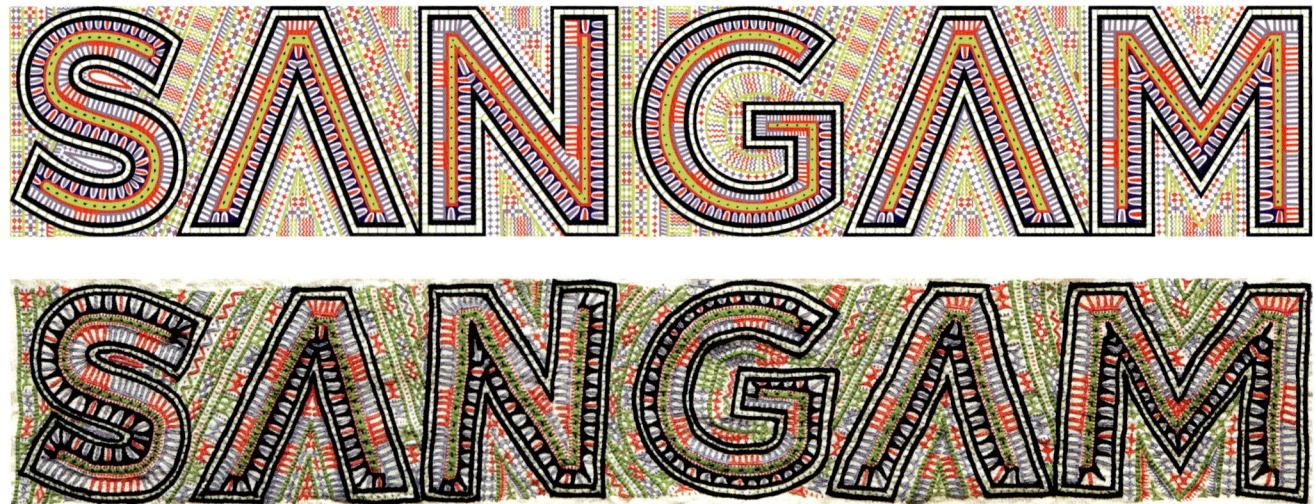

fluid forms and non-geometric structure enabling flexibility in letter formation. The *Sangam* project did not end here: to take it full-circle, Khosla worked with one of the craftswomen, Sajnuben, to physically recreate the letterforms on cloth. The result is a series of capital letters decorated with the shapes typical of *Rabari* embroidery. The spaces between the letters are also filled in, creating a dense patterning that reflects the traditional workmanship of the artisans. The final version of the typeface is a reproduction of the embroidered letters and not the digital reworking, as Khosla deliberately did not want a typeface that looked computer-generated.

For Khosla, working with crafts and artisans is a consequence of having spent a significant period of time in the US. The distance has led to a greater awareness of Indian-ness and a desire, fuelled by a sense of pride, to engage with notions of this. Typecraft aims to create twenty-eight typefaces from twenty-eight crafts from every state in India and is primarily a means of exploring culture and tradition. *Chittara* is part of this project and uses a painterly craft from Karnataka, where the bold graphic forms of these traditional wall paintings lend themselves to letter forms. Typecraft sees a merging of two ideological systems that represent communication. Craft systems contain motifs which have a symbolic meaning or hold value because they are perceived to be part of a long practised tradition. The newly created type form taps into the value-system of craft, of the handmade, of heritage, of a community's skill and knowledge.

Sangam, a typecrafted identity for the Australia India Design Platform.
Designed by Ishan Khosla.
Design and Dehbaria Rabari artisan, Sajnuben from Kukadsar, Kutch, Gujarat 2011.
Photo courtesy
Ishan Khosla Design.

A similar process of exploring indigenous signs and rich cultural heritage is seen in Geetika Alok and Henrik Kubel's typeface commissioned for Wallpaper* Magazine's special India edition, June 2011. Their source of inspiration was *kolam*, the craft of pattern-making where a simple dot grid is marked out on the floor (usually outside the village home) and where coloured powders are used to link the dots and make patterns. Created for celebration, they are ephemeral yet symbolic, contemporary yet traditional. Alok and Kubel have used the grid system, linking dot-to-dot and utilizing the angles created by this process to create a bold contemporary typeface called India.[50] Here, the use of craft as a symbol of identity, transferred to a digital format, is one that shows a progressive adaptation of a tradition, as described by the term *parampara*, rather than a static interpretation. The Handpainted Type project by Hanif Kureshi is another example of the development of type forms through the referencing of traditions and digitization.[51] This project is a means of documenting and preserving the lettering created by vernacular sign painters across India. The process involves tracking down the decreasing number of remaining artists, engaging them in reproducing an entire alphabet in their style of lettering, interviewing them and finally digitally transforming their letterforms into a font that can be downloaded and purchased, with the funding going to the artist. The fonts *Painter Kafeel* and *Painter Suhail* are the first to be released. Digitization enables an engagement with, and a preservation of, a graphic tradition. Himself a graphic designer, Kureshi's appreciation of the vernacular has enriched his own cultural and artistic development.[52]

Rathna Ramanathan has a long-term engagement with documenting ways of writing and approaching scripts. The impetus to do this came from a journey she made across Tamil Nadu in 2003. Seeing the wealth of vernacular sign-writing prompted an instantaneous response to photographically record all that she saw. From the view point of a trained graphic designer and a graphic design historian, the marked reduction of these visual experiences a few years later and the fear of their complete erosion led her to a more focused exercise: documenting how sign writers approach the formation of each of the 247 characters in the Tamil alphabet. Unlike current handwriting practice which teaches that letters have to be formed by moving the pen from one point to the next in a particular order, without raising pen from paper, sign writers approach their craft in a very visual way, with an aim of balancing letters. This is a process that has developed from years of having to communicate

151

India typeface for Wallpaper*.
Illustration by Henrik Kubel
A2-TYPE, 2011.
Image courtesy Henrik Kubel.

Kolam patterns.
Designed by Geetika Alok,
Wolff Olins, 2011.
Photo courtesy Geetika Alok.

Facing page:
India typeface.
Designed by Geetika Alok and
Henrik Kubel, 2011.
Photo courtesy Geetika Alok.

PUTTING DOWN ROOTS: BRANCHING OUT IN MUMBAI AND A LEAFY RETREAT IN DELHI

HOT DESKS AND ROOFTOP POOLS: OUR INDIAN HQ

Our India mission took us, on plane and train, across the sprawling subcontinent, from Ahmedabad to Hyderabad, Jaipur to Puducherry, and Bengaluru to Chandigarh. But we chose **Delhi** and **Mumbai** for our hubs and quarters – a grand and handsome capital and a megalopolis driven by a manic energy. We landed in numbers, keen to hit the ground running. But not before we'd unpacked and settled into a contemporary town house in leafy South Delhi (see page 048) with a palmy, balmy terrace, a grand dining table for communal dhal, rotis and homemade lassi, and a fleet of cars to whisk us – as fast as Delhi traffic allows – to rendezvous. At night we returned to debrief and hit the rooftop pool or find a calm corner for quiet contemplation. In Mumbai, meanwhile, we took a handsome suite of offices conveniently located under the hottest bar and restaurant in the city (see overleaf). Which meant we could bring the party to us, just where we like it. ▶

Wallpaper*

153

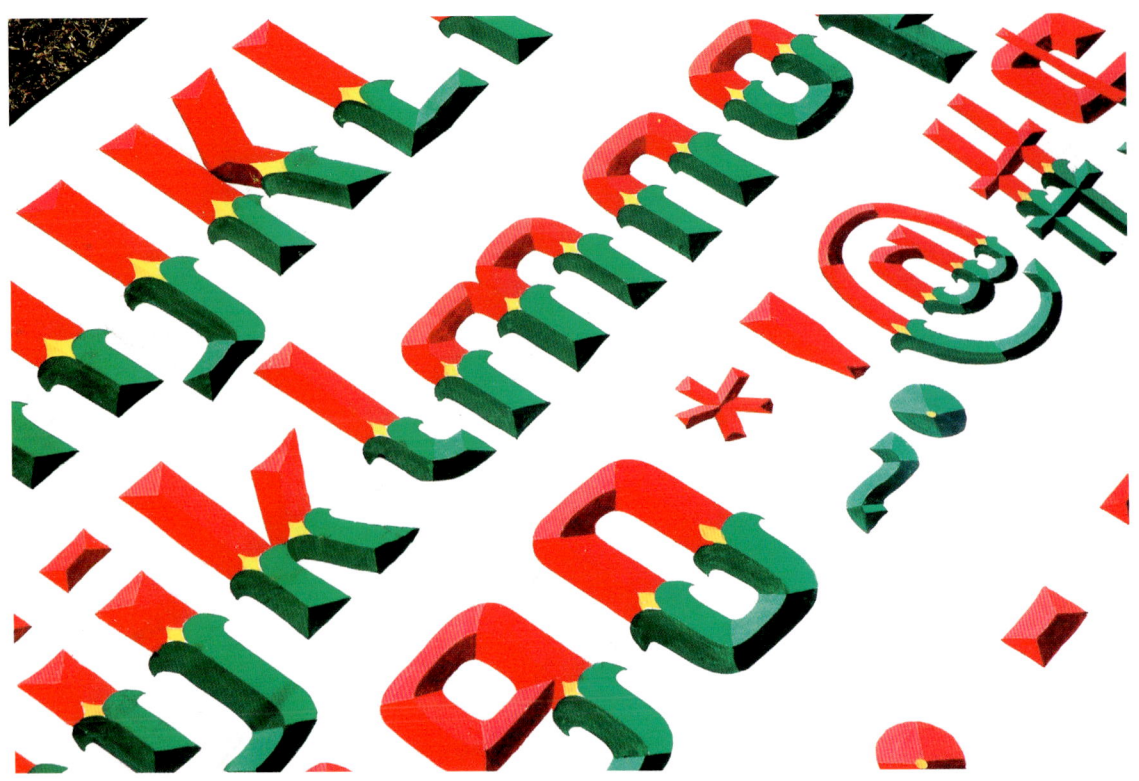

154

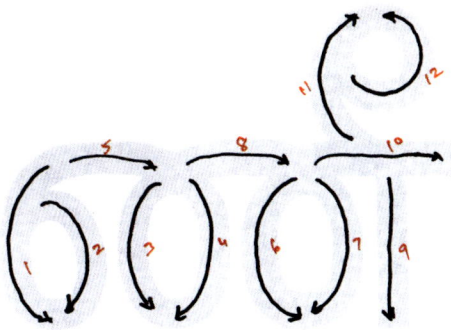

with immediacy, directness, clarity and visual dynamism. The work of un-trained designers is a significant part of the history of graphic design in India. Ramanathan's meticulous recording of each letter, tracing its creation, labelling and numbering the direction of each stroke, will lead to a publication that should prove invaluable to future graphic designers, those developing contemporary typefaces and design historians.[53]

The projects documented here have focused on developments within a number of popular graphic practices by a dynamic group of professional graphic design studios. Their ingestion of international design-approaches and exploration of indigenous forms of expression have resulted in an environment full of visual dexterity, experimentation and inquisitiveness. How this feeds into and affects the broader graphic landscape remains to be seen.

155

GRAPHIC DESIGN: A VISUAL EPILOGUE

The continuously developing dynamism of the graphic design industry is presented here through a range of diverse projects: from exhibition design, to map production, to information graphics, they showcase the great skill and creativity of a number of studios and designers as well as re-enforce the impact of the discipline within a variety of environments.

TURMERIC DESIGN

A Graphic Design and Illustration studio, founded in 2010 by Kriti Monga, New Delhi. Offering a range of graphic design services, their most recent illustrative work is for the Smoke House Deli chain of restaurants.

Identity for Gourmet products, 2009.
Photo courtesy Turmeric Design.

SMOKƎƧUOHROOM

Identity for SHRoom Restaurant, 2011.
Photo courtesy Turmeric Design.

UMBRELLA DESIGN

Creative Communications Company founded in 2004, Mumbai. Run by founder and managing director, Bhupal Ramnathkar and creative director, Karan Rawat, the agency offers a full range of graphic design services.

Recycled Mechanics, 2012.
Creative Director Karan Rawat,
Art Director Uttam Sutar.
Copywriters Sanjay Sure/Sunil Shibad.
Photo Sunil Naik, courtesy Umbrella Design.

R U Films, 2012.
Creative Director Bhupal Ramnathkar,
Art Director Aditi Chaddha.
Photo courtesy Umbrella Design.

VIVEK SAHNI DESIGN

Graphic Design Agency founded in 1993, New Delhi. A well-established company, their most recent venture is in product development and design with a range of ayurvedic beauty treatments inspired by local and global sensibilities.

Kama Ayurvedic Soap box, 2012.
Photo courtesy Vivek Sahni Design.

Kama Ayurvedic Hair treatment, 2012.
Photo courtesy Vivek Sahni Design.

ALOK NANDA & COMPANY

Creative Brand Consultancy founded in 1999, Mumbai. An innovative established, company responsible for contemporary urban brands such as Crossword Bookstore and Barista Lavazza Espresso bar. Filter, a brand and retail space, is their most recent venture.

India in a bar, Filter's range of chocolates flavoured with Indian spices.
Designed by Alok Nanda, Mahesh Ramparia, Ajoy Adavani, 2012.
Photo courtesy Nital Patel.

FILTER

Creative Brand Consultancy founded in 1999, Mumbai. Responding to contemporary urban lifestyles, Filter is their most recent venture, a retail space and in-house brand that integrates the company's creative talents and offers a platform for other graphic designers, photographers, and product designers.

Filter, Retail space, Alok Nanda and Company, opened in 2011, Mumbai.
Photo courtesy Saish Kambli.

INFONAUTS

Information and Graphic Design company founded in 2009, led by Aman Khanna, New Delhi and London. With an international outlook, their information graphics simplify complex information through a clean and strong visual language.

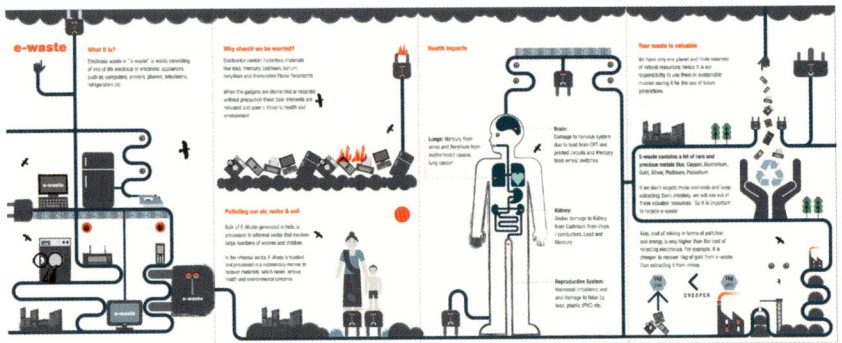

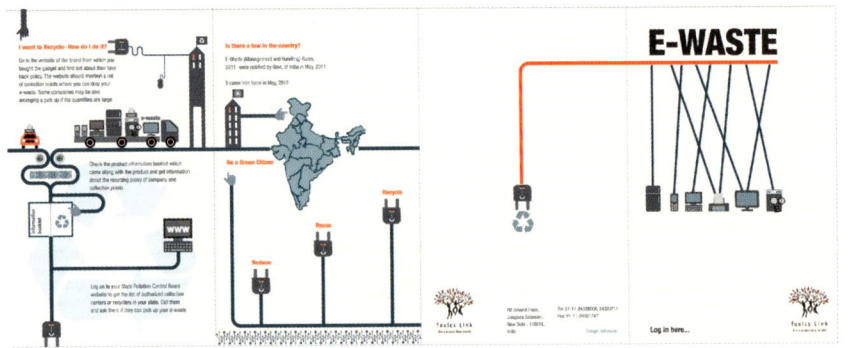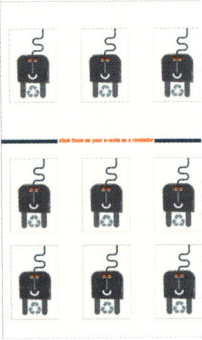

E-waste leaflet for Toxics Link (NGO), 2014.

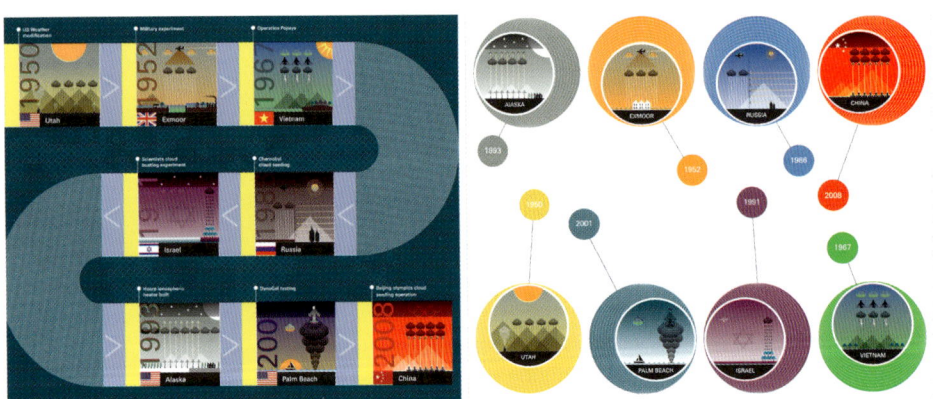

Wicked World Weather, illustration for article printed in *Audi* Magazine, 2010. The charts are an illustrated timeline about weather modification operations lead by different countries. Photo courtesy Infonauts.

JAIKISHAN PATEL AND SNEHAL PATIL

From the Indian Institute of Technology, Industrial Design Centre, Mumbai. Their project illustrates the use of graphic design for everyday need.

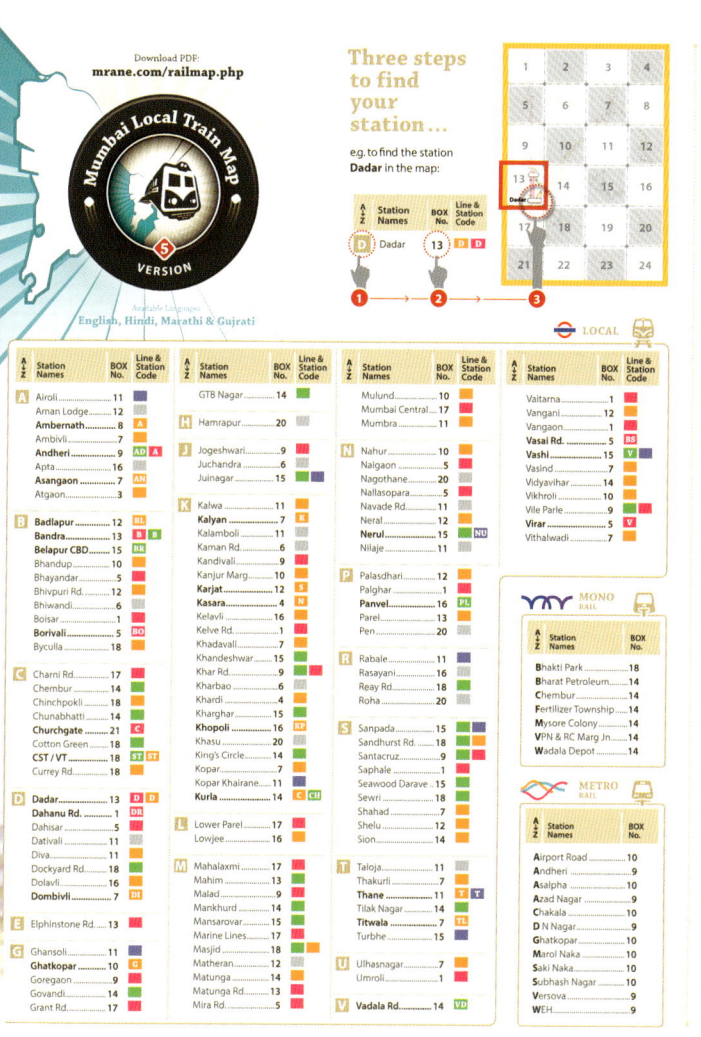

Mumbai Suburban Rail Map.
Designed by Jaikishan Patel and Snehal Patil, 2014.
Photo courtesy Industrial Design Centre, IIT Mumbai.

BOMBAY DUCK DESIGN

Independent Studio founded by Sameer
Kulavoor in 2006, Mumbai. Kulavoor is a
graphic designer, illustrator and visual artist
who is currently making an impact with his
creative work for rock music projects.

NH7 Weekender, unique visual identity, festival logo, stage,
backdrops, bar and posters, badges.
Photo courtesy Zeenat Kulavoor.

TRAPEZE DESIGN

Multi-disciplinary Design Consultancy, founded in 2006, by Ram Sinham and Sarita Sundar, Bengaluru. Integrating a wide range of graphic design services, a culmination of which was best expressed in the exhibition SOAK.

SOAK, National Gallery of Modern Art, Mumbai, 2009.
Photo courtesy Trapeze Design.

INTERIORS IN INDIA

A new generation of design studios and architects are creating an imaginative and diverse range of interior spaces, furniture and furnishings in India. Through the processes of designing, making and marketing, their work is embedded with cultural meaning and engages with issues of locality, sustainability, identity and aesthetics. While the contemporary interior can take many forms, the studios and projects under consideration here are linked through their engagement with craft and the hand-made. Many of them employ India's great wealth of materials, techniques and skilled artisans in traditional ways; while others adopt a non-conventional approach that seeks to broaden our conception of contemporary craft.

Research and documentation of modern and contemporary interiors in India is limited. The photogenic nature of the topic invites image-led publications. Henry Wilson's *India Contemporary* and Angelika Taschen's *Indian Interiors* are filled with beautifully photographed interiors and include basic information on the design ethos of the owners.[1] Daab's *India Design* is purely image-based and covers retail and corporate spaces.[2] However, the most impressive and authoritative body of work is presented in *A History of Interior Design in India* by Muktirajsinhji Chauhan and Kamalika Bose which has focused its first volume on the city of Ahmedabad.[3] It explores interiors, their spatial organization, flooring, ceiling, furniture and furnishings from the mediaeval period to the present day in a systematic and authoritative way. The lack of documentation about interiors underplays the importance of these spaces as repositories of material culture from which future historians and designers can learn about objects, individuals, a society and their relationship to their environment.

Facing page:
Lebua Resort, Jaipur.
Designed by
Urban studios, 2011.
Photo courtesy Lebua Resort.

167

Designers use crafts as a tool of differentiation, to create uniqueness, to add value, to link to a sense of tradition, history and community. The distinction between the professionally trained designer and the skilled crafts person is a historically evolved one. In the past, craft communities produced for rich patrons or for local markets and local needs. They were valued for their ability to create functional items with a sense of aesthetics that had evolved over time and was informed by their knowledge of the user. Post-independence industrialization and urbanization have led to the erosion of these links between the maker and the user. The maker, often based in rural areas, has no understanding of the urban users' needs or tastes. Makers also lack access to education, technology and information which might enable them to cater for urban markets. Today, it is the college-educated, professionally-trained designer who fills the gap between the maker and the market: their knowledge of urban lifestyles becomes the driving force for transporting craft skills into a contemporary environment.

Facing page:
Workshop, Sandeep Sangaru
Bengaluru, 2011.
Photo courtesy Divia Patel.

CRAFTED FURNITURE

The use of craft skills in the creation of interiors and products for interiors has been employed by designers for generations. Two of the most successful contemporary studios in this field are AKFD and Viya Home. Both companies describe their work as being 'modern in aesthetic and rooted in tradition', yet they cater for very different markets. AKFD, run by Ayush and Geetanjali Kasliwal, was launched in 2006 in Jaipur, Rajasthan.[4] Taking their inspiration from, and working with, the wealth of craft communities within the region, their designs are characterized by an aesthetic that is a reflection of simple quotidian modernity, linked to heritage but often with a humorous twist. Their wooden furniture range, for example, was inspired by the common daybed, the charpoy, which has a lathe-turned frame and woven surface. Their design consists of a wooden frame strung with ropes of leather across the seating and the back support. The leather straps are the same as those used to turn the mechanism of the manual sewing machine. The stark and utilitarian aesthetic is a reminder of the modernist furniture of the 1950s in India, a legacy of Le Corbusier as seen in Ahmedabad or Chandigarh.[5] AKFD's popular series of lamps are inspired in their form by the elegant shapes and patterns seen in Mughal architecture. Their relatively large scale gives them a majestic sense of presence and when lit they cast evocative patterns across the walls. Their grandeur is, however, a clever illusion as it obscures the fact that they are made from simple birdcage wire. In addition to these two ranges, Ayush Kasliwal engages with a wide body of crafts people through an exploration of a large range of materials and techniques for products which include woven dhurries, carved wooden storage jars, brass diyas, and marble tables.

The production processes behind such a range reflect cultural and economic shifts and need to be documented as evidence of this period of rapid national transition. AKFD have a dual level of production, incorporating both village and factory production, that enables them to meet the demands of internal and export markets. Their factory in Jaipur is where the procurement of raw materials is centralized and where they have woodworking and finishing facilities and can monitor the quality of the finished products. Their wooden furniture range illustrates the long and complex process which incorporates craft communities and the factory environment. The wood is procured and sorted in the factory.

Facing page:
Leather-strap furniture.
Designed by Ayush Kasliwal
for AKFD, Jaipur, 2007.
Photo courtesy David Dunning.

171

It is then sent to the *kharadis*, the communities who traditionally turn wood. The lathe-turned pieces are bought back to the factory where the framework for the furniture is manufactured. Finally, the leather straps, sourced from Kanpur, the centre of the leather industry, are woven into the furniture to complete it. AKFD argue that the 'mundane work (is) accomplished by machines and the intelligent design and production conceived and executed by the human mind, hand and spirit'.[6] The company's extremely successful range of lamps is, by way of contrast, produced entirely in the village of Sultana in Rajasthan, which has a population of some seven hundred families, most of whom are dependent on metal craft. Utilizing their knowledge of metal, AKFD introduced wire wrapping to the community. They were taught how to adapt a technique normally used to make birdcages into making lamps and items of furniture.[7]

The production process of the lamp has been documented by AKFD. They have produced a booklet which locates the village, describes the surrounding infrastructure, the status of the craftsperson, the work environment, the properties of iron, the processes of four different techniques, the tools, the sources of local raw materials and their costs, photographs of the traditional products made from these techniques and some of AKFD's newer products. It provides an introductory guide to any other entrepreneur who wishes to use the same artisans.[8] This form of data collection is a legacy of the NID of which Ayush is a graduate and where students are trained to appreciate the importance of documentation. This confers a greater sense of value, substance and strength of meaning to the products. The company employs approximately four hundred people directly and indirectly and they want their products to reveal 'strong empathetic bonds with the craftspeople involved and a reverence for the lineage of the craft.'[9]

By way of aesthetic contrast, Viya Home founded by Vikram Goyal and Divya Goyal seeks to transform high-end interior spaces from a rather anonymous, internationally-inspired minimal aesthetic to one with an elite Indian identity. Influenced by the grandeur of palaces, and by the concept of craft patronage exercized by the maharajahs, their crafted furniture, lighting and decorative objects are dramatic sculptural statements that re-interpret traditional motifs and forms and have an aesthetic of handmade opulence. Signature designs include the metal-crafted Finial Collection, inspired by Mughal architecture, and the

Facing page:
Wire Lamps.
Designed by Ayush Kasliwal for AKFD, Jaipur, 2007.
Photo courtesy David Dunning.

173

Hundred Petal Lotus collection, as well as the beaten lotus stool and dome lighting, all made by metal craftsmen using complex chasing and repoussé skills. Their opulent design aesthetic generates commissions from those with a similar visual language, such as established fashion designers Rohit Bal, and Tarun Tahiliani. Their commissions, often large scale, recreate a contemporary regal splendour for shop interiors, hotels, and homes.

The reliance of designers on craftspeople who work with them often leads to long-term personal relationships. Viya Home have nurtured such a relationship with two metalworking mastercraftsmen over the last eight years. Satpalji, now 88, and Ajmalji, 44, are both from families with a tradition of metalcrafting and are employed exclusively for Viya Home. The designers work closely with the craftsmen from the initial conception of the design, through experimentation with technique, material and pattern, to the final product. The process is mutually educational. Vikram Goyal describes the relationship as being one 'based on mutual trust and collaboration. We value their expertise, the craftsmanship and input into design and production; they value the consistence of work and employment and the satisfaction of having skills stretched from time to time.'[10] The success of the business has enabled the master craftsmen to move from working in their homes to workshops outside of Delhi, some of which are self-owned. They have created skilled clusters that have a division of labour differentiating between processes such as chasing, hammering, and finishing. Viya Home has also recently started working with Kauser, a 29-year-old second-generation artisan who has begun to develop his own cluster. Long term engagement has involved assisting the craftsmen with their personal finances and other general support, which has led to their becoming more self-sustaining. However, despite their success, their legacy is still uncertain. Within the family, the sons who have access to education wish to explore options beyond metal crafting. This is illustrative of a systematic pattern of change: the demands of contemporary businesses require displacement from village-based production into workshops and factory environments. Designer-led revivals and contemporizing of craft traditions have achieved pockets of success in preventing the loss of skills, but, even in these instances, it may only be for the short term. Success is filtered into educating the next generation and often their aspirations lie beyond that of localized craft production, desiring instead the higher incomes and

Facing Page:
Finial Collection.
Brass, repousse and
chasing technique.
Designed by Viya Home, made
by Mohd. Ajmal Khan, 2006.
Photo courtesy Viya Home.

Left:
Workshop
Viya Home, Delhi, 2007.
Photo courtesy Viya Home.

Right:
Beaten Lotus Table.
Brass, hammering technique.
Designed by Viya Home, made by
Ramesh Anand, 2007.
Photo courtesy Viya Home.

177

Interior of Anantaya.
Retail space for AKFD, Jaipur, 2004.
Photo courtesy AKFD.

more comfortable lifestyles of urban-based professions, consequently implying fundamental changes to society and culture.[11]

The success of both companies is based on a sense of Indian-ness that is embedded in their work through the process of designing, making, and marketing. A study by Hannerz and Löfgren, of the globally successful retailer IKEA, argues that it sells furniture through its Swedish-ness (which is defined by order and cleanliness) and, reciprocally, Swedish-ness through its furniture. This commodification of the 'essential' qualities of a nation suggests that a commodity has the power to mobilize and shape national identity.[12] Similarly, AKFD and Viya Home are successful because they sell Indian-ness through their products and products through their Indian-ness. However, they do sell different versions of Indian-ness: AKFD promote the handcrafted nature of their products, deriving an Indian identity and authenticity from this: 'The revival of ancient skills, which are then adapted to the modern world's growing needs for functional yet beautiful objects, has become the AKFD trademark....Every meticulously crafted object that bears the AKFD brand name, no matter the material, can be traced back to an artisan working in the traditional environment of the *karkhana* or the workshop.'[13] Their promotion actively centres on preservation and innovation and the adaptability of craft to a contemporary environment. Their commitment to and inspiration from the craftsperson is referred to extensively in their five-page press release. In contrast, Viya Home's marketing focuses predominantly on the creation of a luxury brand, deriving authenticity from designs that reference the opulent cultures of the Mughal emperors and the maharajahs. For many of Viya Home's affluent consumers, the desire to recreate a luxury aesthetic overrides any associations to the craftsperson. Viya's promotion of the handmade element is understated. A rare instance in which it was highlighted was in their 2011 association with Odegard, a New York based company known for their championing of handmade, sustainable products. For their international customers, therefore, who are perceived to be more interested in these issues: 'Odegard and Viya Home come together to celebrate exquisite craftsmanship, the preservation of generations old skills and traditional communities and the shared belief that beautifully made objects can speak to a higher level of awareness, appreciation and compassion'.[14] AKFD also have a thriving international business, with a strong list of companies who have stocked their lines or for

179

Interior of Good Earth, Mumbai.
Photo courtesy Good Earth.

whom they provide access to craft-skills. They actively promote the global element of their company.

AKFD and Viya Home have their own retail outlets, which enable the appropriation of these 'Indianised' lifestyles. Other spaces for the consumption of Indian-ness for the home include Good Earth, a chain of stores founded by Anita Lal. The first outlet opened in 1996 in Mumbai, with expansion to Delhi, Bengaluru and Chennai happening only in 2006 after the liberalization of the economy and a noticeable rise in consumer purchasing power.[15] The company has established a reputation for craft-focused quality home products such as linens and tableware. They position themselves as an 'Indian design house that celebrates the culture and history of a rich and diverse land' with their core values of sustaining tradition and ecology. They sell an essentialist vision of India that defines the home through themed collections entitled Lotus, Golconda, Vrindavan, Modern Mughal, and India Modern amongst others.[16] The collections have an aesthetic that is based on a selection of historic themes and iconic motifs. Dynamism in pattern and colour are more prevalent than a minimal modernist chic.

A range of different aesthetics which link contemporary urban living to India's traditions are offered by independent boutiques such as Bungalow 8, Design Temple, and Le Mills in Mumbai, Cinnamon Store in Bengaluru and Cochin as well as the Craft Council store in Delhi. Bungalow 8 mixes antique with modern, Le Mills sell a European aesthetic through select Indian craftsmanship, and Design Temple, with the introduction of a range of furniture, lighting and rugs in 2011, continue to disseminate their very elegant urban design language. Such lifestyle stores are relatively new in India; most emerged after 2006 and play a significant role in constructing a cosmopolitan identity for India. Facilitating consumption from these stores and integral to the design environment are magazines on architecture and interior design. These include *Elle Décor*, established in 2000, *Architectural Digest*, with its first issue printed in 2012, and *Domus* India in 2011.

Studio Wrap, founded by Gunjan Gupta, also focuses on the revival of craft techniques to create luxury furniture. The use of materials such as silver and precious stone define her work. Her promotional material emphasizes the connection of luxury, craft and design. The Silver Linings collection is typical in its use of material, form and craft skills. Hand-

carved by stone masons from Jaipur, these three-dimensional irregular rhomboids are constructed from granite tiles, creating a six-faceted form accented with a simple lining of pure silver at the bottom. Their shiny surfaces reflect the environment around them. These blocks are utilized as coffee-tables. Their form acts as a blue print for subsequent creations in which Gupta uses mosaics of coloured stones on the surface. Much of Gupta's furniture consists of sharp, graphic, angled shapes, cubes, rhomboids and pyramidal structures that are made in her combined studio, workshop and showroom outside of Delhi.[17] Her most iconic piece so far is the Bicycle Throne. This conceptual seating is based on ideas around recycling, which are particularly strong in India, and is inspired by the ubiquitous bicycle-vendors, the men who transport goods, piled high on the backs of their cycles, from one destination to another. The chairs were originally conceived during the Experimental Design Project at Droog in Amsterdam in 2008, where Gupta used recycled bicycle parts and entitled the project 'cyclerecyclecycle'. Developing the idea further, her newly hand-crafted, well-made thrones come in three versions which are differentiated by their cargoes: a stack of fabric, a load of rice sacks or a pile of rolled bedding. An extension of this idea can be seen in the Family Bench which consists of stools made from bicycle wheels and joined together to provide multiple seating. Stools made from recycled bicycle wheels are a common sight in India where, as an example of *jugaad*, they represent the ingenuity and resourcefulness of a non-waste culture. Their familiarity on the streets of India makes these pieces resonate with links to the everyday.

Recycling and resonance with the vernacular are the basis for the Katran range of chairs designed by the Sahil and Sarthak Design Company. Sahil Bagga and Sarthak Sengupta coined the trademark 'Zero Kilometer design' which is applied to a number of products they developed for a project that required them to furnish the interiors for the Lakshman Sagar resort in Raipur, Rajasthan. The architects were Vasant and Revathy Kamath, known for their eco-friendly sensibilities. In keeping with this ethos, the project required that the furnishings be made from local resources and skills. Thus, their range of furniture and products brings together a quirky mix of crafts and skills sourced from the nearby villages, towns, and cities. Eye-catching and vibrant, the Katran chair is constructed from recycled fabric rope wound around an elegant high-backed metal framework. The metal sculpted form combined with the random colours of the sari-rope, knotted together, creates an appealing

185

Facing page:
Kapda Bicycle Throne.
Designed by
Gunjan Gupta, 2008.
Photo courtesy
Gunjan Gupta.

Clockwise from top:
Stools made from recycled
bicycle parts, Jaipur, 2011.
Photo courtesy Divia Patel.
Bicycle Family Bench.
Designed by Gunjan Gupta, 2008.
Photo courtesy GunjanGupta.
Bicycle carrier, Jaipur, 2011.
Photo courtesy Divia Patel.

Clockwise from top:
Local market waste,
Barmer, Rajasthan, 2012.
Process of weaving Katran
Chair, Studio, New Delhi, 2012.
Weaving of waste into balls of
fabric, Barmer, Rajasthan, 2012.
Photo courtesy Sarthak Sahil
Design Co.

Facing page:
Katran Chair.
Designed by Sarthak Sengupta
& Sahil Bagga, 2009.
Photo courtesy
Sarthak Sahil Design Co.

roughness. The rope is made from the off-cuts of brightly coloured georgette saris and other material discarded as waste by export houses and factories. Used by local people as a cheaper alternative to jute or coir, the sari-rope can be found woven across the common charpoy.[18] Here it provides an interesting and powerful example of contemporary vernacular design. Its use in furniture is therefore not a new technique. Other designers have adapted the charpoy, creating smaller benches or stools where the ropes are woven around simple wooden frames, versions of which are sold through international retailers Zara Home and Apostrophe in 2011. The Katran range is made using the skills of three sets of people: the local blacksmith who makes the metal framework, the farmers and their wives who make the coloured ropes, and the people who weave the rope around the metal frame.

The success of the range has meant that the company have opened a workshop in Delhi where they can monitor the production process. The ropes are still sourced from Rajasthan but the range has been developed to include different shapes of chairs and lighting, adapting the metal framing accordingly. Clients can choose different colour-ways and textures of rope to suit their interiors. The studio's work has been showcased in Milan and other European design fairs where it was enjoyed for its colour and sustainability story. Sahil and Sarthak are also exploring other strands in keeping with their design philosophy. Experimentations with the black pottery of Manipur, a region in the Northeast of India, have resulted in interesting prototypes of a lamp and tea set, and they continue to develop new ideas.

CRAFTING SUSTAINABILITY: THE STORY OF BAMBOO

The story of bamboo is one of the most fascinating to emerge in the field of furniture design in India. In this instance, Indian-ness is defined by a local approach to a complexity of issues concerned with environmental, social, and cultural sustainability. At a time when these issues are being addressed globally, the manner in which designers in India approach them is of relevance to designers beyond India. Sustainability has been a part of design pedagogy at the NID since its formative years. Inspired by Victor Papanek's *Design for the Real World* and E.F. Schumacher's *Small is Beautiful*, generations of designers were taught to appreciate that the power of design is about the creation of solutions that improve the lives of, and seek to empower, India's vast body of people who have access to very little.[19] NID's engagement with bamboo should be seen as a precursor to the now commonly referred to process of 'design thinking'. International literature on design theory such as Buchanan's *Wicked Problems in Design Thinking* shifted attention away from purely object-based exploration towards a more generalized concept of 'design thinking' that could be used to derive solutions for processes and systems.[20] Following this, Tim Brown's *Change by Design* and Tom Kelly's *The Art of Innovation* advocated a more 'human centered' design process which integrated designers with communities, encouraged a collaborative process involving a diverse range of specialists and promoted systemic thinking.[21] The development of such a holistic approach that looks beyond the aesthetics of a product and that acknowledges anthropological and sociological insights in design is a fundamental aspect of the bamboo story.

International interest in bamboo tends to be periodic and focuses on its qualities as a sustainable material. It has a rapid growth cycle making it highly renewable, it is able to regenerate without replanting, it prevents soil erosion and its forests produce high levels of oxygen. For designers it offers a material that can be light and flexible and has the tensile strength of steel. The ability of designers to translate this into a dynamic range of contemporary products can be seen in often limited edition pieces such as Tejo Remy and René Veenhuizen's Bamboo Chair, J.P. Meulendijk's LOCK table or, most importantly, Jair Straschnow's experimental Grassworks Collection.[22] These designs successfully shift the perception

Cube Stool made from bamboo.
Designed by M.P. Ranjan,
craftsman fabricator,
Brajendra Debbarman, 2002.
Photo courtesy
Deepak John Mathew, NID.

193

Katlamara Chalo Workshop, at
Katlamara, Western Tripura, 2005.
Photo courtesy M.P. Ranjan.

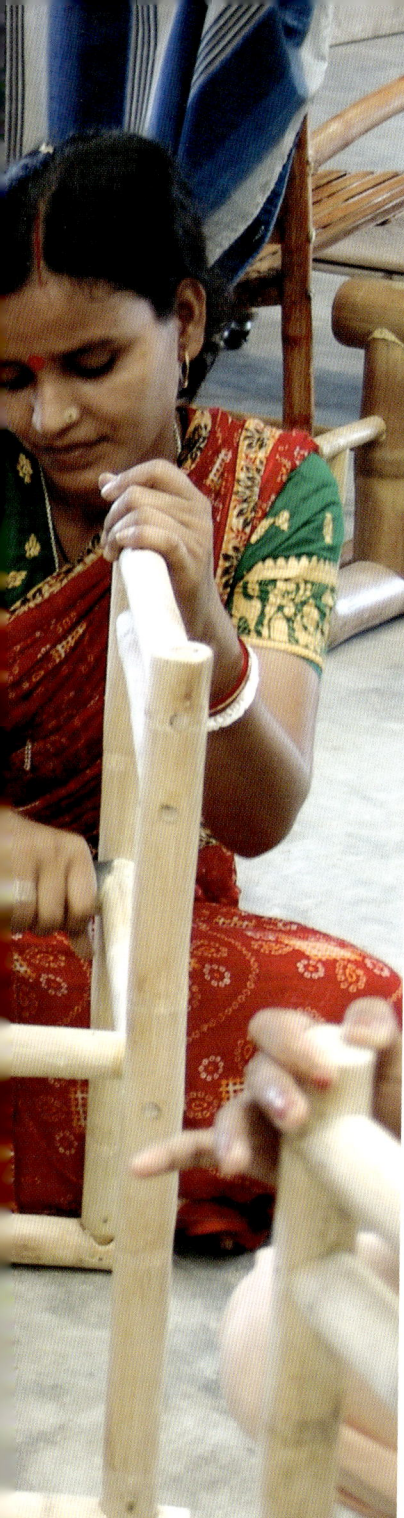

of bamboo away from the exotic, low-cost, bad quality associations of the past. Their clean minimal aesthetic repositions bamboo products as eco-friendly, stylish and perfect for 21st century lifestyles.

India's contribution to this field, despite the long-term engagement with it, tends to be omitted from design literature, often because it has little access to or exposure in international design fairs and festivals, or because design-led stories that focus primarily on aesthetics might consider them as derivative or less sophisticated and therefore not comparable. However, this omission ignores the deeper and more complex issues surrounding sustainable design. India's work with bamboo tackles the holistic definition of sustainable design, one that addresses economic and social sustainability and attempts to empower groups of artisans in rural India to become self-sufficient. Many young Indian designers have undertaken projects that aim to alleviate poverty through design interventions. They take their inspiration from the seminal work of Professor M.P. Ranjan, former head of the Centre for Bamboo Initiatives at NID, whose association with bamboo began in the 1980s prompted by observations made during an extensive study of craft production in Northeast India.[23]

A series of workshops held in the state of Tripura highlighted a set of problems that were typical of the craft sector and explained the underdevelopment of the area: artisans lacked an awareness of the range of techniques and processes available to them and the entrepreneurial spirit to innovate and diversify their own product range. The remoteness of the region, the difficulty and expense of transport, meant that the craftspeople were too distant from urban markets to be able to communicate with it, neither were they able to develop an awareness of contemporary urban needs, let alone aesthetics, in order to respond to those markets. The workshops were held with the aim of training and up-skilling craftspeople and providing them with contemporary, relevant designs for products from which they might generate more income than their limited production of baskets and small items of everyday use. During the workshops designers and craftspeople together worked on the prototypes and learnt from each other, after the workshop these prototypes would be left with the communities to use, adapt, take into production, and sell anyway they liked. The greater objective was to educate and empower the communities to establish their own entrepreneurial

195

units. Resulting from these workshops is a series of product prototype collections from which two of the key designs are the cube stool and the folding chair.[24]

The Cube Stool, developed in 2002 at a workshop by M.P. Ranjan, is an example of a design solution that has taken into consideration the implications of working with a rural craft community. Simplicity is at the core of the design, both in terms of its contemporary aesthetic and its construction. It uses local material, local skills, and locally available technology. The primary material is bamboo splits that are easily made at the common facilities centres, a unit which houses simple tools and machinery available for use by the whole community. The machines are easy to operate and allow splitting into uniform cross-sections. These are then prepared and can be fitted together by hand in small production units in the surrounding villages. During the process a specially designed metal-clip was developed to facilitate the joining of the bamboo splits. The cube can be adapted to other shapes or can be fitted with fabric seating, as well as back and arm rests to enable a variety of products to be made. The system is decentralized and labour intensive to encourage the use of hand-skills and a greater labour force.[25] The folding chair was part of a product range developed in 2005 at the Katlamara Chalo workshops. Some forty craftsmen and women were trained to build a

Unassembled 'Organic Chair' showing its component parts. Designed by M.P. Ranjan, craftsman fabricator, Manna Roy with Katlamara team, 2005. Photo courtesy Alekh Ajayaghosh, National Institute of Design.

Facing page:
'Organic Chair', Katlamara, Tripura.
Designed by M.P. Ranjan, craftsman fabricator, Manna Roy with Katlamara team, 2005. Photo courtesy Alekh Ajayaghosh, National Institute of Design.

Glimmerfly.
Designed by
Andrea Noronha, 2009.
Photo courtesy Xavier D'Silva.

Facing page:
Bo Lamp.
Designed by
Andrea Noronha, 2009.
Photo courtesy Xavier D'Silva.

range of twenty-five products, all of which could be made using three simple tools available to the remotest of craftsmen. According to the project report, the design solutions developed could equip a rural home with good quality furniture at a very reasonable price. The chair is illustrative of the two key features developed during this project: the Katlamara joint and a system for the construction of knock-down furniture which makes it easier to transport the furniture to local and national markets. The knock-down element reduces the chair to six key parts which can be easily reassembled.[26]

Guidelines developed over the years have influenced the next generation of designers to instil a set of aspirations in their products: they aim to develop the existing skills of the local people, creating a sense of pride. Their products have to be simple in construction and aim to use a minimal tool set and limited hardware; the variety of material used in one product has to be limited and sourced locally. The designs have to be appealing and affordable to a local market but also

be adaptable to a more sophisticated urban environment. The work of Andrea Norhona, a student at the NID in 2009, illustrates the complexity of the design and production process within such an environment.[27] Her designs for the Glimmer Fly lighting and the Bo lamp demonstrate her skill in projecting a sophisticated aesthetic that utilizes the identity of the bamboo, retaining its characteristic grain, knots, and nodal features. This is rare in an international arena where the majority of designers achieve their stylish, contemporary pieces by using laminated bamboo boards that iron out the identifiable characteristics of the material leaving a clean minimal wood-like appearance.

The Glimmer Fly lamp has a striking visual randomness to its form which is constructed from bamboo splits of different sizes. These can be made by hand or, if larger quantities are required, a simple machine can be used. Bending the splits to create a curve is done through heating them using a blow torch and then shaping them around an MDF jig supplied by the designer. The splits are joined together using a brass strip and

199

rivets. The simple Bo lamp is carved from one section of a bamboo pole, known as the culm, which is defined by the nodes at either end. The culm is thinned and gracefully curved to give an elegant form to the lamp. The wiring passes through the thinned out section to the LED light fitting. Of the two designs, the simplicity of the Bo lamp, made from a single piece of bamboo, suggests ease of production. However, it requires a greater degree of skill to manufacture than the Glimmer Fly: each piece is unique as each bamboo culm varies in length and width and is dependent on the eye of the maker, requiring a highly-skilled craftsman with independent aesthetic judgement to make the elegant form – the defining feature of the lamp. LED light fittings also require resources that are not available in a village setting.

The Glimmer Fly can be manufactured more easily with less skilled craftspeople and is therefore the most viable option for the craftsmen to incorporate into their repertoire to generate income. The lamp has the versatility to have a horizontal or vertical configuration and further variations of form can also be made without changing the production process thereby giving them the opportunity to make their own adaptations to the design. Sightings of the lamp in a restaurant called Crepeteria in Pune, part of a chain, suggest some success in meeting the set of guidelines and having the products reach beyond the NID and Tripura. Unfortunately, like most of the other bamboo products, they have not reached their full market potential. Andrea is currently working on taking the more complex Bo lamp into production.[28] Other designers too have experimented with bamboo in similar workshop environments; for example, Siddhartha Das has designed a dynamic series of woven bamboo lamps which express a local-global aesthetic but which too have not entered the market place through lack of supporting governmental or commercial structures.

Two designers who are continuing M.P. Rajan's legacy and taking the bamboo story into the future in a more sustained manner are Rebecca Reubens and Sanjeev Sangaru. Reubens runs Rhizome, a social design firm that advocates a holistic approach to sustainability. Her aim is to create a workable social entrepreneurship model for the Kotwalia community, an indigenous tribe based in Gujarat, dispossessed from its land and struggling for survival. A three-way partnership between Rhizome, the Tapani Bamboo Development Centre, and the Eklavya Foundation has led to the development of a four-year training

Facing page:
Woven lamp.
Designed by
Siddhartha Das, 2011.
Photo courtesy Siddhartha Das.

Bamboo Canopy, exterior.
Design Studio and Retail space
designed by Rebecca Reubens
and Errol Reubens, 2009.
Photo courtesy
Rebecca Reubens.

202

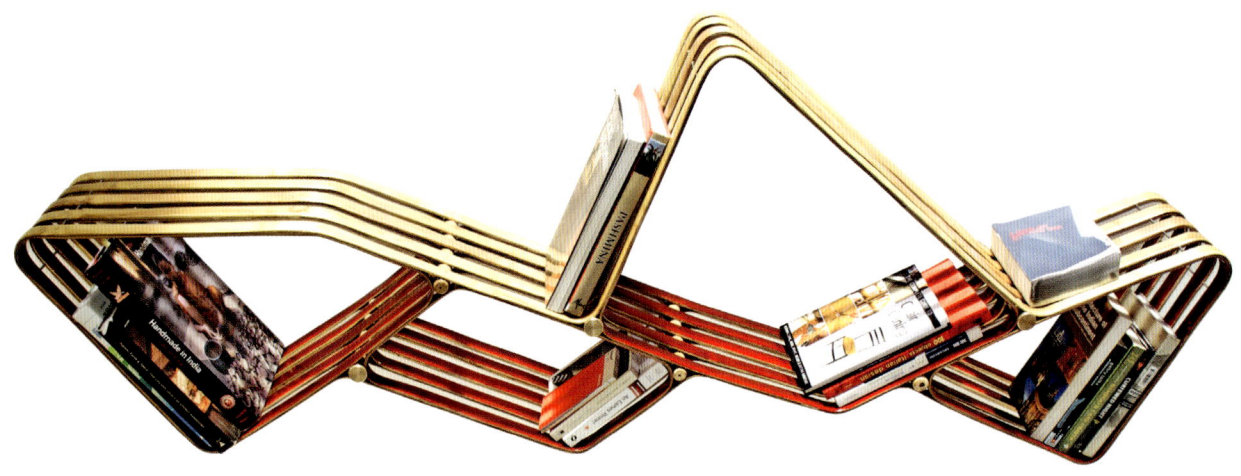

programme. This focuses on up-skilling of the craftsmen from the beginners level, with basic training in using tools, to an advanced level which results in a student being able to read and implement design drawings. The most tangible aspect of Reubens' enterprise is Bamboo Canopy, a retail outlet designed with the assistance of her architect brother, Errol Reubens. Lined on the exterior with rows of bamboo and fitted in the interior with custom-made bamboo lighting and screens, the shop is an evocative space perfectly suited to showcasing a range of bamboo products. From stylish recliner chairs to cute rocking horses, from table lamps to multifunctional seating and shelving units, the products represent the work of a number of designers and serve to highlight the beauty and utility of bamboo to prospective buyers. Orders taken via the shop are then executed by the trained Kotwalia craftsmen.[29]

Sanjeev Sangaru is the most commercially and conceptually successful of a new generation of young designers experimenting with the material in innovative ways. With a degree of commercial success and orders from international clients, his studio is bridging a gap between the local and the global. The studio, based in Bengaluru is staffed by trained crafts-people from Tripura, many of whom would have attended the NID workshops.[30] Their continued employment and empowerment through design is a vital part of the legacy of the bamboo story. Sangaru's furniture range is entitled Truss-me and is based on his experiments with the tensile strength of bamboo. A truss is an architectural term

204

which refers to a triangular shape that lends support to a structure. By splitting a bamboo pole to a point just beyond the node and laminating the joint with another piece of split bamboo from the inside, Sangaru constructs a simple triangular frame that is lightweight yet able to bear heavy loads. This single module has become the key component in his designs. His inventive seating system shows how the multiplication of this simple triangular form can be used to create a visually striking piece of public seating. The bench is fitted together within an unobtrusive steel framework which makes the bamboo look elegant and dynamic. The concept of the truss is taken further in his storage units, which are a step beyond the average utilitarian bookshelves. Here the triangular forms are expanded into larger elongated angular shapes that are brought together into one irregular whole. These asymmetric configurations are evocatively named: thus, Landscape appears like a series of floating hills when mounted seamlessly on the wall, and Tree spreads its branch-like structure out above its base of trunk-like bamboo poles. Like the unconventional shelving units of designers such as Ron Arad, these pieces are functional as well as eye-catching installations. The studio has also developed a dynamic range of furniture and toys for children. Sangaru's work has a strong contemporary aesthetic which does not aim to project an Indian identity. Its universal appeal was apparent in the 2011 Beijing International Design Triennial where it was showcased alongside other bamboo designs from East Asia and Europe. The core value and aspiration for his studio are 'Local materials with local skills to make global products'.[31]

Facing page:
'Landscape' shelving.
Designed by Sandeep Sangaru,
2010.
Photo courtesy Sandeep
Sangaru.

Above:
Truss Me Bench from the Truss
Me Collection.
Designed by Sandeep Sangaru,
2009-10.
Photo courtesy Sandeep
Sangaru.

Dis-locating/Globalizing Craft

To design furniture that is rooted in the local but with a universal appeal is at the heart of two international design practices with connections to India: that of Satyendra Pakhalé, based in Amsterdam, and Doshi Levien, based in London, both of whom produce for international clients. While many designers use craft as a signifier of locality, these designers celebrate its potential for hybridization and as a positive symbol of globalization.[32] Hybridity across multiple cultures, between craft and technology, connecting the manufactured with the handmade is fundamental to their work. This is a continuity of tradition that is not based on a sense of nostalgia; it is a shift into the contemporary that adds value and recognition to craft.

Bold, linear, graphic detailing with an elegant range of colours is what draws the eye to the sensual experience of Charpoy: a range of day beds by Doshi Levien which combines the tactility of the hand-made with the utility of the industrially produced.[33] Charpoy contains a layered narrative, one with multiple meanings, identities and connections which express the dynamic flow of global and local forces. In its associations to an archetypal piece of Indian furniture there is a layer that links to the vernacular and a national identity that is to be found in everyday objects. Through the careful and detailed embroidery and appliqué stitching on the mattress,

Facing page:
Charpoy.
Designed by
Doshi Levien, 2007.
Photo courtesy
Alessandro Paderni.

Above:
Detail of Charpoy showing hand-stitched signatures.
Designed by
Doshi Levien, 2007.
Photo courtesy
Alessandro Paderni.

207

a group of crafts women based in Ahmedabad express a layer of their Gujarati heritage. That their names are embroidered on the edge of each mattress reveals their identity to the consumer and, more fundamentally, it confers a sense of authorship and value to their work, which is not part of the craft tradition in India. Strong emotional, personal, and cultural connections are conveyed through the accompanying cushion range entitled 'tools of inspiration' and their depiction of quotidian tools used for the everyday rituals of cooking, sewing or making chai, as well as objects with links to the designers such as a computer fan found in Manhattan or an Alessi tape dispenser. The use of khadi with its associations to the nationalist movement adds a further layer of meaning.[34] Moreover, mattresses facilitate connections: laid out on the floors in Indian shops they invite customers in, to sit, to talk, to spend time interacting, to view and buy; they are spaces for social and commercial engagement. Through their use of a graphic representation of *chaupur*, a game of dice, counters and chequered board, in the centre of the mattress, the Doshi Levien's Charpoy invites participation and social connection.[35]

Facing page:
My Beautiful Backside.
Designed by
Doshi Levien, 2009.
Photo courtesy
Alessandro Paderni.

Above:
Loyly (sauna) with Ananda
(personal spa).
Designed by
Doshi Levien, 2011.
Photo courtesy Marco Viola.

Italian industrial production is used in the sleek geometric yet fluid lines of the CNC machine-cut wooden base, which is balanced by the sensuality of the black-lacquered coating. These layers reflect the hybrid identity of the studio. Nipa Doshi and Jonathan Levien, both trained at the Royal College of Art in London. Doshi is of Indian origin and also studied at the NID. Hailed as a successful British design studio, their work is influenced by their backgrounds but not to the point where it becomes constraining. Their great variety of projects is evidence of the cosmopolitan nature of their studio: from My Beautiful Backside, a sofa that takes its inspiration from an Indian miniature painting and uses hand embroidered Indian fabric, to Ananda, a personal spa, and Loyly, a sauna, both designed for the Italian company Glass. Their work reflects their desire to 'un-define' design, to move away from constraining identities and expand the references used in the design world which are all very Eurocentric.[36]

Satyendra Pakhalé's work ranges from industrial design to limited edition pieces and includes furniture, radiators, tableware, and ceramics. He has designed products for many prestigious companies

209

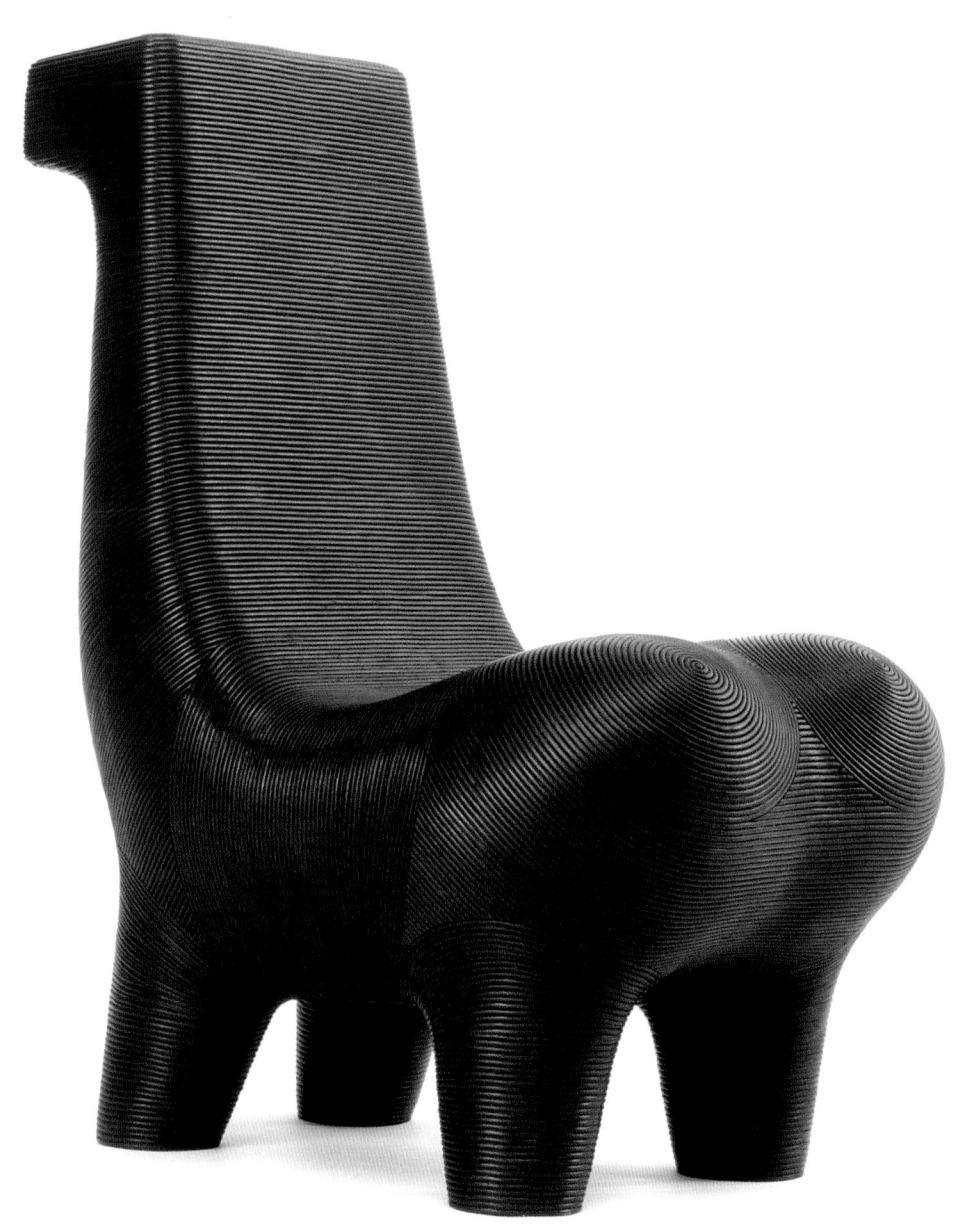

Facing page:
B.M. Horse Chair.
Designed by
Satyendra Pakhalé, 2000.
Photo courtesy Gabrielle
Ammann Gallery, Cologne.

Above:
B.M. Horse Stool.
Designed by
Satyendra Pakhalé, 2008.
Photo courtesy Gabrielle
Ammann Gallery, Cologne.

including Alessi, Morosso, and Cappellini. Pakhalé's BM Horse chair and stool represent a seven-year obsession that began in 2000. Following a series of assignments which focused on technological design, Pakhalé felt a desire to address the lack of human content and cultural context in design. He returned to India where his explorations into a variety of crafts including pottery, woodcraft and metalcrafts enabled him to engage with the experience of the handmade, of craftsmanship. The technique of *dhokra*, a lost wax process using bell-metal, was to become his passion for the next seven years. Working with the craftsmen of Washim, Pakhalé learnt the process through creating a series of small bowls and vases. The technique leaves a distinctive linear raised metal-thread patterning across the entire object. This is the result of wrapping thin strands of beeswax around a clay mould of the desired shape. The wax is then covered with another layer of clay. Firing and pouring molten metal in between the layers of clay melts the wax and leaves the final form. The next four years Pakhalé spent travelling back and forth from India attempting to scale up the process to produce larger pieces of furniture. Multiple failed attempts led him to shift production to Europe in 2005. Here, to replicate the striated effect of the *dhokra* technique, he found a form of plastic piping which could be squeezed from a silicon gun onto a full scale model of the chair. 3D scanning and digitization were used to study how the molten metal would flow over such a large surface. The final version was cast in an Italian foundry used to casting modern sculpture.[37]

211

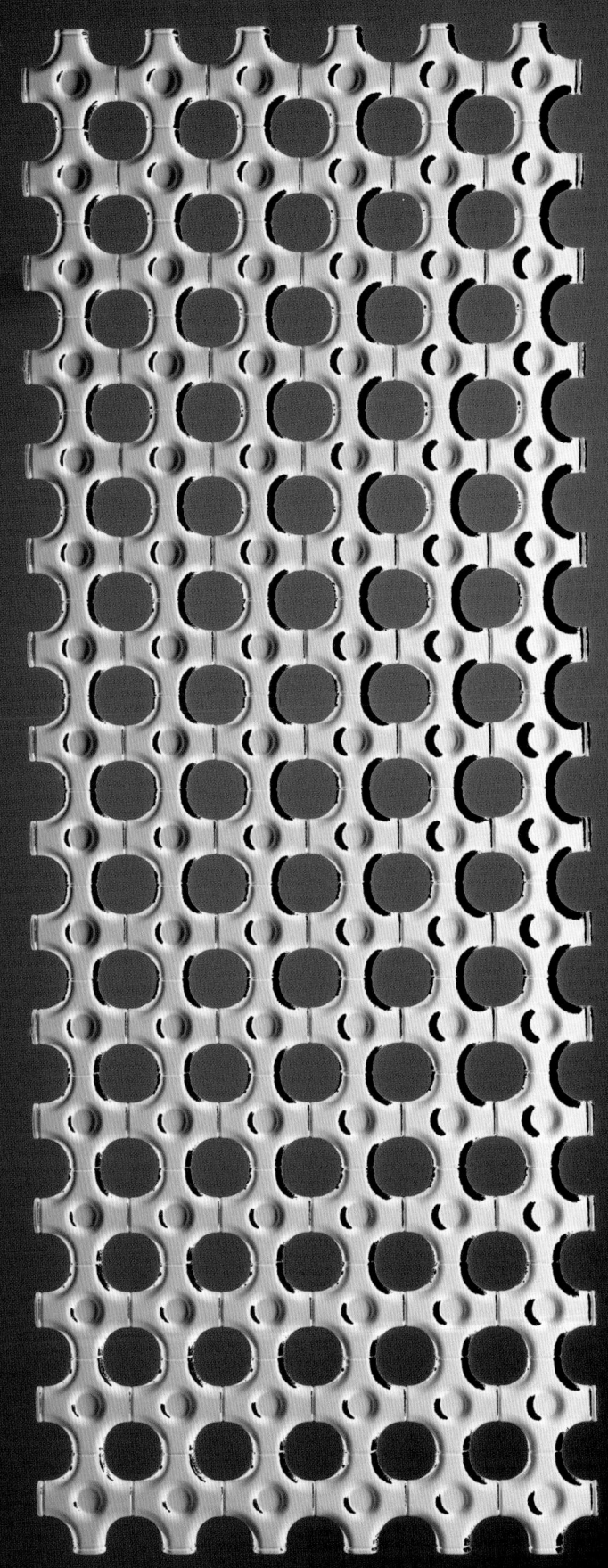

Thus, the result is a limited edition series which is a beautiful and extraordinary realization of the synthesis of new materials and technology, with a craft tradition dating back thousands of years. The pieces possess a strong sensual physicality defined by striated metal piping which elegantly accentuates the curves and bulbous forms. In this reconstruction of the visual characteristic of the *dhokra* technique, Pakhalé recognized the proximity of the 'tribal' aesthetic to the contemporary aesthetic. Similarly, the form of the horse chair takes inspiration from the votive terracotta horses of Bankura, West Bengal, which are characterized by their rounded structure, elongated necks and short legs. Exposure to such a rich visual and material language is evident in Satyendra's work, not overtly but through gentle referencing, which keeps it grounded to a cultural context and rooted to the local. Like Doshi Levien, the diversity of this designer can be seen in his wide range of products. The Add-on radiator, in particular, is a clever utilitarian and aesthetically pleasing example of his industrial pieces.

These studios have given Indian craft a contemporary global relevance. The plurality of references and ideas embedded in their work make them project 'familiarity and newness'.[38] Their work promotes respect for craft, valuing it and using it to give emotional and cultural worth to industrial design. For these designers, it is by looking in from the outside, by seeing India from another part of the globe, that they are able to it use craft skills with such powerful effect.[39]

213

CRAFTED INTERIORS

The projects considered here are an amalgamation of interiors that are designed by studios for existing buildings and those that are created by architects as integral to their own buildings. Hotel environments in particular use 'crafted' links between past and present; as places of transition they offer 'experiences' of the local within a sanitized and otherwise globalized uniformity. The most distinctive developments in this field include two hotels for the Lebua group, Devi Garh and Devi Ratn.[40] Devi Garh, a luxury resort in Jaipur, was hailed as a triumph of contemporary design when it opened in 2000. Its success was in restoring the grand shell of an 18th-century building but creating interiors that were modern in feel, with a simple clean aesthetic. White walls and discreet interventions of painted or inlay-work with semi-precious stones on accent walls convey a re-invented tradition for its association to heritage but with a minimalism that would have been unfamiliar to its 18th-century owners. This was the vision of owners Lehka and Anupam Poddar and a team of architects and designers which included Gautum Bhatia and Rajiv Saini. Devi Ratn is a second venture by Anupam Poddar. Here the contemporizing of tradition is seen in the newly-built outer structure as well as in the interiors. Designed by Aniket Bhagwat, the building takes its inspiration from the geometry of the architectural astronomical instruments of the Jantar Mantar in Jaipur, an 18th-century observatory built by Maharaja Jai Singh II. The bold structure creates interesting public spaces, including a circular dining hall that has an almost industrial starkness and the drama of beams of light mimicking the astrolabe. There is austerity and abundance.

It is with the interior spaces that Pronit Nath and Amish Nath, of Urban Studio, were able to explore a language of contemporaneity that goes beyond white-box minimalism and take as its starting point Jaipur's long tradition of jewellery-making and gem-craft. Translated into the theme of *nav ratn*, the nine gem stones that are linked to cosmic energy and the body, the vibrant colours of the *nav ratn* are used to create opulence that is resonant of the maharajas' palaces of earlier centuries. Each room has a different colour, each with detailing that combines several traditions, each of which has had its own layer of contemporization: traditional

Facing page:
Room inside Lebua Resort.
Designed by
Urban Studio, 2011.
Photo courtesy Urban Studio.

215

mirror embellishment as found in historic Rajasthani palaces is transformed into an acrylic mirror and *thekri* glass geometric configuration creating a band or 'necklace' that winds its way through the rooms. Striking chevron patterning across the floors has been inspired by traditional *leheriya* textile patterns. Jali screens, perforated stone-craved ventilation and shading devices have always lent themselves to re-interpretations as they are the most adaptable of architectural features, easily modernized while always linked to the past. Here, they are used in the large-scale construction of entire walls allowing for the maximization of lighting effects.[41] Other hotels which continue this dialogue between past and present through crafted luxury include Raas Jodhpur, designed by Lotus in 2011.

Private homes also offer spaces for contemporary visualizations of craft applications.[42] Rajiv Saini, one of the architect/designers who worked on the Devi Garh project, has created spectacular interiors using traditional craft techniques. Many of his interiors use rich luxurious materials, stone and marbles to create an opulent modernity. The use of wood inlay or marquetry is another avenue for his exploration of materials and technique; from the minimal and abstract inlaying of lines of dark wood across walls of pale wood that hide built-in wardrobes to the more complex and pictorial use of marquetry across entire walls to create the defining feature of a room. With the marquetry room Saini was answering a brief in which he had to develop a space that was suitable for a private collection of contemporary folk art. His response was to explore the potential of craft techniques, of which marquetry was one. Traditionally practised in south India and used mainly for the tourist trade on small-scale items like decorated wooden boxes, the up-scaling of this technique to cover the entire surface of a wall several metres in length and height, and extending across the ceiling and floor, was a complex exercise. It required detailed drawings and much sampling of wood. A series of panels was created in the craftsmen's studio and then brought together in the final space. Problems with wood expanding and contracting in different environments had to be factored in for the finished effect to be one of an all-encompassing wooden tapestry. The pattern of palm trees on the walls and the grass on the floor echoes the client's garden, which can be seen through two glass walls. It brings

the outside inside. The modernity of the glass box is balanced by the warmth of the wood. It is in the juxtaposition of techniques and material that a contemporary aesthetic is achieved. Saini regularly employs craft techniques and the mixing of textures and materials for this effect.

217

Crafted interior, private home.
Designed by Rajiv Saini
and Associates, 2006.
Photograph by Ken Hayden,
courtesy Rajiv Saini
and Associates.

219

LOCALIZING THE GLOBAL

A very different approach to craft, one that is not based on the reproduction or re-invention of an Indian craft aesthetic, but is focused instead on sensitivity to the environment, offers a powerful form of localization, one that has been championed by Bijoy and Priya Jain and their architectural practice, Studio Mumbai'.[43]

A short film captures the rhythmic movement of a skilled craftsman as he applies muted green plaster across a wall, his attention focused on making fine and defined strokes. Another short film, only a few seconds long, records the grace and practised skill with which a young woman picks up and carries hand-made bricks. These films form part of a visual library of local skill and ingenuity recorded informally by Bijoy Jain and other members of Studio Mumbai as they go about their daily work. They demonstrate an acute sensitivity to the environment which feeds into their built structures. They offer a very different approach to craft, one where it is experienced through 'the quality a building can evoke' through its materiality, tactility, site specificity, and sensuality – it should be 'something magical that lives and breathes.'[44]

The Studio team includes a large group of skilled crafts people who are nurtured and trained internally and are central to its success. A visit to their practice in Alibag, Mumbai, immediately coveys the commitment to traditional skills, local materials and local building techniques. Here in the open air, the designing, modelling, full-scale mock-ups, experimenting with materials, and fine tuning are carried out. The craftsmen are given notebooks in which they sketch their own ideas and solutions. A library of their red-inked drawings, measurements and working solutions is steadily growing.[45]

The Studio is interdisciplinary, incorporating architecture, landscape, interior design, and furniture. Palmyra House was their first big commission and shows the harmonizing of the interior with the exterior. It is a family retreat set within a functioning coconut grove beside the Arabian Sea, with the trees providing shade and shelter and being a determining factor in the design. The house consists of two rectangular structures sitting slightly angled but

Facing page:
Interior of Palmyra House, Alibag.
Designed by Studio Mumbai, 2007.
Photo courtesy Divia Patel.

221

222

almost parallel to each other; they are made of wooden slats which allow the air to circulate through. Inside, there is brushed plaster on the walls in muted grey/green tones. The interior is defined by its sharp clean lines and beautiful surface-finishing, with the combinations of materials and textures creating a handcrafted, understated elegance. The light fittings and furniture are in keeping, very minimal, very functional. Studio Mumbai is a practice that is sensitive to global flows, but is rooted in place. They use craft and local construction techniques to create a modernist aesthetic – a spirit which is manifested throughout their work.[46]

Exterior of Palmyra
House, Alibag.
Designed by
Studio Mumbai, 2007.
Photo courtesy Divia Patel.

223

GLOBALIZING THE LOCAL

Global thinking and the desire to transcend national definitions is the premise of many studios practising in India today. Serie architects, founded by Chris Lee and Kapil Gupta, are an international practice with a base in India, China, and the UK. Tote on the Turf in Mumbai was their renovation of a colonial building requiring transformation into a banqueting hall, restaurant, and bar. Much of the interior structure for the building takes its inspiration from the mature rain trees outside the building which are a distinctive part of the historic race-course environment in which the Tote stands. Thus the interior of the lounge bar is covered with a stunning walnut wood veneered panelling which is constructed from rhomboid shapes intricately joined together to create a three-dimensional faceted appearance. The panelling forms a series of trees with intersecting branches and has channels of bronze tracing out the tree patterning. The process of designing and construction is an amalgamation of technology and craft skills. CAD and 3D modelling tools were employed to map out a system for the coordination of the panelling, which was assembled by skilled craftsmen from Rajasthan, using fairly primitive tools. The high level of finish achieved by the crafts people along with an aesthetic based on straight lines give the project a contemporary feel.[47]

Within a section of the Tote there is a stunning steel canopy of multiple branches emanating from tree-like structures that provide the support for the roof. They cleverly and intentionally mimic the mature rain trees outside. The complex web of branches, as well as acting as a truss for the roof, is the system which divides the internal spaces for their different functions. To ensure precision, the steel web was laser-cut but the sections were assembled and welded together by boiler fabricators, as they were capable of more precise work then steel fabricators. According to the architects, 'the success of the installation is that the final product conceals the fabrication method and appears to be a system of curved sections.'[48]

The Busride Design Studio, founded by Ayaz Basrai, has used craft skills to mimic high-end, technology-simulating interiors in their restaurant and bar project named SHRoom. Located in Delhi, in a

building near the heritage site of the Kutb Minar, the SHRoom is a futuristic looking space catering for the conspicuous spender, consumers who want to be seen in global spaces. Inspired by the form of the mushroom, the interior is elegant and all-white, its drama comes from the graceful curves, smooth surfaces and organic forms that constitute the furniture, the bar and the patrician screens that define the internal spaces. The global aesthetic projects a high-tech construction method. However, rather than relying on technology the entire space is hand-carved from MDF. There is no use of computer-aided machines enabling easy and precise shaping and cutting of wood. What could, from a western perspective, be seen as an interesting 'reversal' of method is a creative adaptation drawn from necessity, a resourcefulness that

Exterior of Tote on the Turf,
Mumbai.
Designed by
Serie Architects, 2011.
Photo courtesy
deGustibus Hospitality.

comes from dealing with limitations (in this case, of technology) and is an Indian trait worth recognizing and preserving.[49] In another venture, they have parodied the trend for using extravagant budgets to create soulless interiors, by reversing the methodology and asking how a limited budget can lead to spaces that tell stories and have a soul. Thus, in a series of restaurants called Smoke House Deli, the décor consists exclusively of hand-drawn details. Carvings, mouldings, objects and pictures are all hand-drawn onto walls, shelves and cabinets, creating an illusion and fusion of two-dimensional and three-dimensional elements. They create narratives through incorporating local themes and found objects. The limitations of budget have led to interesting interiors and a celebration of the illustrators' skill.

Interior of Tote on the Turf,
Mumbai.
Designed by
Serie Architects, 2011.
Photo courtesy
deGustibus Hospitality.

227

Bar at Tote on Turf, Mumbai.
Designed by
Serie Architects, 2011.
Photo courtesy
deGustibus Hospitality.

Craft, in its mutability, offers designers and architects an infinite potential for expressing a multiplicity of meanings through their furniture and interior spaces. The environments they create enable the consumption, appropriation or experiencing of local, global, and cosmopolitan identities.

Smoke House Deli,
Phoenix Mills, Mumbai.
Designed by The Busride
Design Studio, 2011.
Photo courtesy
The Busride Design Studio.

INTERIORS: A VISUAL EPILOGUE

The constant inventiveness of architects and designers in shaping visually stimulating interiors is presented here in a diverse range of projects. They illustrate the continued construction, whether hand-made or industrial, of an aesthetic that embodies the cosmopolitan lifestyle explored in this book.

SAMEEP PADORA & ASSOCIATES (SP+A)

Architecture, Urban Design, Planning. Founded in 2006. Their work looks beyond tradition, challenging existing typologies through the re-interpretation or a building or a design process in the context of contemporary culture in India.

Indigo Deli @ Palladium, Parel, Mumbai, 2011.
Designed by Pankaj Mhatre, Shreya Poddar, Vinay Mathias.
Photo courtesy Himanshu Chowdhry.

ROOSHADSHROFF

A multi-disciplinary design and research studio, founded in 2011, Mumbai. This studio operates in the fields of architecture, furniture, product design, graphic design, and fashion. It explores new ways of working with craft and hand-skills to create contemporary urban furniture and interiors.

Christian Louboutin Boutique, Horiman Circle, Mumbai, opened 2013.
Design architect, 212 Box from New York.
Interior application by ROOSHADSHROFF,
Photographer Ritam Banerjee.
Photo courtesy Christian Louboutin.

Detail of embroidery technique on wood used for the interior walls. Developed and patented by the ROOSHADSHROFF.
Photographer, Ritam Banerjee.
Photo courtesy Christian Louboutin.

232

EVERYDAY PROJECT

A design project uniting furniture, products and graphics, founded in 2012 by Ajay Shah, Mumbai.
This retail space is defined by a fresh, modern and clean aesthetic.

Shop designed and curated by Ajay Shah, 2012.
Photo courtesy Mrigank Sharma, Indiasutra.

INDUSTRIAL PLAYGROUND

Furniture design, founded in 2009 by Ajay Shah Design Studio, Mumbai. An ethos of simple, functional, industrial design is at the heart of these furniture designs.

Right:
Other Side, 2012.
Photo courtesy Everyday Project.

Below:
Axis, 2013.
Photo courtesy Everyday Project.

KHOSLA ASSOCIATES

Architects and Interior Design firm, founded in 1995, Bengaluru. A team led by Sandeep Khosla and Director Amresh Anand. Local-Global sensibilities are integrated in many of their interior projects, often incorporating graphic design services from TSK Design.

Tower Kitchen, UB City Towers, Bengaluru, 2013.
Collaboration between Khosla Associates and TSK Design.
Photo courtesy Amit Pasricha.

JOSMO STUDIO

A furniture design studio, founded in 2010 by Anjali Mody, Mumbai. A studio which makes quirky custom pieces drawing inspiration from everyday life. It incorporates minimal, modern and traditional influences and strives to adopt sustainable practices at every stage of production.

Box Coffee Table, 2012. Photo courtesy Sayantoni Palchoudhuri.
Below: Bari Bookshelf, 2012. Photo courtesy Sayantoni Palchoudhuri.

EN INDE

Anupama Sukh Lalvani, founder/creative director and Sonal Sood, co-founder of en Indie, a jewellery brand (founded in 2004) and retail space, opened in 2012, New Delhi. Their work is influenced by both rural tribal elements as well as the urban and industrial.

en Inde, retail space, Meherchand Market, New Delhi. Designed by Anupama Sukh Lalvani, 2013. Photo courtesy Sonal Sood.

CONCLUDING STATEMENT

There is a need to construct a design history for India, to build upon existing research and to excavate further into the vast and diverse field that constitutes the term 'design'. A better documented history can illuminate our understanding of the effects of design practice on the shaping of environments and societies over time, as well as situate India's differences and strengths more firmly within the global discourse. However, assembling such a history is a formidable task: the enormous wealth of information from different levels of society, regions, and time periods is inestimable. Thus, this study, in charting the creativity of a small group of designers within the context of post-1990s economic liberalization and globalization, is offered as one component of a much broader narrative.

NOTES

INTRODUCTION: INDIA 2000

1   For example: "India Goes Global," *The Times* Focus Report, August 14, 2007. Also, "A bumpier but freer road", *The Economist*, September 30, 2010. Also, "India's surprising economic miracle," *The Economist*, September, 30, 2010.

2   For an overview see Christiana Brosius, *India's Middle Class: New forms of Urban Leisure, Consumption and Prosperity* (New Delhi: Routledge, 2010).

3   See Christopher Pinney, "Colonial Anthropology in the 'Laboratory of Mankind'," in *The Raj: India and the British 1600-1947*, ed. Christopher Bayly (London: National Portrait Gallery publications, 1990), pp. 252-263. For an overview of how architecture and landscape were documented see Maria Antonella Pelizzari, ed., *Traces of India* (Montreal: Candian Centre for Architecture, 2003). For the mapping of India see, John Keay, *The Great Arc* (London: Harper Collins, 2000).

4   Sunil Khilnani, *The Idea of India* (London: Hamilton Hamish, 1997), pp. 150-195.

5   Rahul Mehrotra, *Architecture in India since 1990* (Germany: Hatje Cantz, 2011), p. 30.

6   Jawaharlal Nehru, Inaugural Address, in Seminar on Architecture (Delhi: Lalit Kala Akademi, 1959); cited in Kazi K. Ashraf and James Belluardo ed. *An Architecture of Independence* (New York: The Architectural League of New York, 1998), p. 14.

7   Ravi Kalia, *Chandigarh in Search of an Identity* (Carbondale: South Illinois UP, 1994). Also, Peter Blake, *Form Follows Fiasco: Why Modern Architecture hasn't worked* (Boston/Toronto: Little, Brown and Co., 1977).

8   For an interesting series of photographs of Delhi Modernism by Madan Mahatta see www.frontlineonnet.com.

9   Kazi K. Ashraf and James Belluardo ed. *An Architecture of Independence* (New York: The Architectural League of New York, 1998), p. 14.

10 Jawaharlal Nehru, Inaugural Address, in Seminar on Architecture (Delhi: Lalit Kala Akademi, 1959) sited in Kazi K. Ashraf and James Belluardo ed. *An Architecture of Independence* (New York: The Architectural League of New York, 1998), p. 14.

11 Partha Mitter, *The Triumph of Modernism: Indian artists and the avante-garde 1922-1947* (London: Reaktion Press, 2007). Also, Geeta Kapur *Contemporary Indian Artists* (Delhi: Vikas, c1978).

12 Kavita Singh, "Mulk Raj Anand: A Visionary Aesthete," in *2000: Reflections on The Arts of India*, ed. Pratapaditya Pal (Mumbai: Marg Publications 2000), p. 20.

13 Advertisement in Marg, vol 2, no.2, February 1948.

14 H. Kumar Vyas, *Design in India: An exhibition designed for the Festival of India in Britain, 1982* (Ahmedabad: National Institute of Design, 1982). See

also Singanapali Balram, *Thinking Design* (Ahmedabad: National Institute of Design, 1998), p. 19 and pp. 27-46.

15 Gandhi's ashram is also viewed as having the spirit of modernism, see Rahul Mehrotra (2011), p. 24.

16 In 1930 Lakshidas Ashar, a political supporter in Gandhi's ashram re-designed the wheel, simplifying it, making it horizontal rather than vertical and therefore more portable. The Yeravada Charka, as it was known, meant that Gandhi could continue the symbolic act of spinning wherever he went, even in jail. H. Kumar Vyas. (1982). Also Singanapali Balram (1998), p. 19. For an account of Gandhi's re-design of a national cap see Emma Tarlo, *Clothing Matters* (London: C. Hurst & Co., 1996), p. 82.

17 Radhika Singh, *The Fabric of Our Lives: The Story of FabIndia* (India: Penguin, 2010), pp. 16-17.

18 See Abigail McGowan, Crafting the Nation in Colonial India (New York: Palgrave MacMillian, 2009).

19 Mulk Raj Anand, editorial to *Homage to Handloom*, Marg, vol.15. no.4 (1962): 2

20 Hermann Goetz, "The Calico Museum of Textiles at Ahmedabad," *Marg*, vol.3, no.4 (1949): 58.

21 K.G. Subramanyan, "Contemporary Design developments in Handlooms," *Marg*, vol.15, no.4 (1962): 42.

22 Papul Jayakar, editorial to *Homage to Handloom*, Marg, vol.15. no.4 (1962): 3.

23 Subrata Bhowmick, "How it all Began", *Pool Magazine* 6 (2010): 14.

24 Charles Eames and Ray Eames, *The India Report*, 1958 (Ahmedabad: National Institute of Design).

25 For the colonial impact on art education see Saloni Mathur, *India by Design: Colonial History and Cultural Display* (Berkeley: University of Californiam 2007). See also Saloni Mathur, "Charles and Ray Eames in India," Art Journal, vol.70. no.1 (2011): 34-53.

26 For personal accounts see interview with Kumar Vyas in "Rock Solid: Foundation of Industrial Design," *Pool Magazine* 12 (2011): 11-14. For interview with Dashrath Patel see "Design Vs Styling," *Pool Magazine* 6 (2010): 4-5.

27 H. Kumar Vyas, *Design: The Indian Context* (Ahmedabad: National Institute of Design, 2000).

28 See Ashoke Chatterjee, "Design in India: The Experience of Transition," *Design Issues*, vol.21, no.4 (2005): 4-10. Also, Uday Athavankar, "Design in Search of Roots: An Indian Experience", *Design Issues*, vol.18, no.3, (2002): 43-57.

29 Victor Margolin, "A History of Design and the History of the World", *Journal of Design History*, vol. 18, no. 3, (2005), pp. 235-243.

30 See Wil Arts, "Through a Glass Darkly: An Introductory Essay", in *Through a Glass Darkly, Blurred Images of Cultural Tradition and Modernity over distance and time,* ed. Wil Arts, (Netherlands: Brill, 2000), pp. 1-9. Also Dilip Gaonkar, "On Alternative Modernities", *Public Culture*, vol 11, no.1 (1999) pp. 1-18.

31 Kamala Ganesh and Usha Thakkar, eds, *Culture and the Making of Identity in Contemporary India* (New Delhi: Sage, 2005), pp. 21-24.

32 Eric Hobsbawm, and Terence Ranger, eds, *The Invention of Tradition* (Cambridge: Cambridge University Press, 1983).

33 Jyotindra Jain, "Indian 'Folk Art': Tradition, Revival and Transformation", in

2000: *Reflections on the Arts of India*, ed. Pratapaditya Pal (Mumbai: Marg Publications 2000), p. 66. For a fuller discussion of Parampara, see Kapila Vatsyayan, "From Interior Landscapes into Cyberspace: Fluidity and Dynamics of Tradition", in Kamala Ganesh and Usha Thakkar, eds, (2005), pp. 39-50.

34   K. Vatsyayan, "From Interior Landscapes into Cyberspace: Fluidity and Dynamics of Tradition", in Kamala Ganesh and Usha Thakkar, eds, (2005), p. 40

35   "India Goes Global", *The Times* Focus Report, 14 August 2007.

36   For example, Christiana Brosius, *India's Middle Class: New forms of Urban Leisure, Consumption and Prosperity*. Also, Nirmalya Kumar, *India's Global Powerhouses* (Harvard Business Press, 2009). Also, Pavan K. Varma, *Being Indian* (India: Penguin, 2004). Also, Amartya Sen, *The Argumentative Indian* (India: Penguin, 2005).

37   Paul Hopper, *Understanding Cultural Globalization* (USA: Malden, 2011) p. 35

38   Different terms for these processes have been offered by many theorists. Arjun Appadurai's work has been particularly influential in this field. He has articulated globalization as a series of 'scapes' which cut across national boundaries, interconnect in multiple and differing contexts: thus the flow of people is termed 'ethnoscapes', technology 'technoscapes, information 'mediascapes', ideas and ideologies as 'ideoscapes' and money 'financescapes'.

39   Referred to and discussed as 'Impatient capital' by Mehrotra, Rahul, 2011. See also Ibrahim Mostafa Eldemery, "Globalising Challenges in Architecture", *Journal of Architecture and Planning Research*, vol 26, no 4, (2009): 343-354.

40   Kamala Ganesh and Usha Thakkar, eds, (2005), p. 21

41   Roland Robertson, one of the key theorist on this subject, refers to this as a process where the 'universal is particularised and the particular is universalised'. As summarised in Paul Hopper, (2011) p. 98. As a case study see also Alison Goodrum, *The National Fabric: Fashion, Britishness and Globalization* (London: Berg, 2005).

42   For an overview of theories of Globalization and Cosmopolitanism see Paul Hooper (2011), pp. 157-179.

43   Guy Julier, "Locating Design Cultures" (paper presented at the Premsela Design Cultures symposium, UV Amsterdam, 25 May 2011). See also Guy Julier, *The Culture of Design* (London: Sage Publications, 2008).

44   For a historical perspective of Hauz Khas see Meher Castelino, Fashion Kaleidoscope (India: Rupa Publications, 1994), pp. Also Emma Tarlo, (1996), pp. 288-294.

45   For tradition as located in village India, see Jyotindra Jain, "Indian 'Folk Art': Tradition, Revival and Transformation", in *2000: Reflections on The Arts of India*, ed. Pratapaditya Pal (Mumbai: Marg Publications 2000), p. 66. For an analysis of how national identity can be located in popular culture see Tim Edensor, *National identity, Popular Culture and Everyday Life* (Oxford: Berg, 2002).

46   For an explanation of the term see C.K. Prahlad, *Fortune at the Bottom of the Pyramid* (New Jersey: Pearson Education, 2005). The range of literature on this subject includes, L.K. Sharma and Shobit Arya, *The India Idea* (Wisdom Tree, 2011). Also, Navi Rajdou, Jaideep Prabhu and Simone Ahuja, *Juggard Innovation*, (San Francisco: Jossey-Bass, 2010). For Systems design see

projects by interdisciplinary studios such as Centre for Knowledge Studies, Delhi or Quicksand, Delhi & Bengaluru.

47 For a summary of some of these events see: Ruchita Madhok, "The rise of the Design Event", in Online magazine *Perch*, 7 August 2012. www.perchontheweb.com.

48 *National Design Policy*, (Ahmedabad: National Institute of Design, 2007).

FASHION IN INDIA

1 Shefalee Vasudev, *Powder Room: The Untold story of Indian Fashion* (India: Random House, 2012).

2 Meher Castelino, *Fashion Kaleidoscope* (India: Rupa Publishing, 1994).

3 Michael Boroian and Alix de Poix, *Indian by Design: The Pursuit of Luxury and Fashion* (Singapore: John Wiley & Sons, 2010). Also, Shefalee Vasudev, *Powder Room: The Untold story of Indian Fashion* (India: Random House, 2012).

4 Abu Jani and Sandeep Khosla, *India Fantastique* (London: Thames and Hudson, 2012).

5 Emma Tarlo, *Clothing Matters* (London: C. Hurst & Co., 1996). Also, Mukulika Banerjee and Daniel Miller, *The Sari* (Oxford: Berg, 2003). Also, Dulali Nag, "Fashion, gender and the Bengali middle class". *Public Culture*, vol.3, no.2 (1991): 93-112. Also, Naseem Khan, "Asian Women's Dress: from Burqah to Bloggs – changing clothes for changing times", in *Chic Thrill*, ed. Juliet Ash and Elizabeth Wilson (London: Pandora Press, 1992), pp. 61-74.

6 See Ritu Kumar, *Costumes and Textiles of Royal India* (London: Christie's books, 1999). Also G.S. Ghurye, *Indian Costume* (Bombay: Popular Book Depot, 1951).

7 For a summary of fashion theories see Yuniya Kawamura, *Fashion-ology: An introduction to Fashion studies* (Oxford: Berg, 2005).

8 For a discussion of fashion theory and the exclusion of non-western fashion systems see Jennifer Craik, *The Face of Fashion: Cultural Studies in Fashion* (London: Routledge, 1993), pp. 1-43.

9 See Emma Tarlo, *Clothing Matters*, for her use of Bourdieu's theory on class and taste, as a tool with which to explore the way the Indian elite have, in recent history, used 'strategies of distinction' to differentiation themselves from the west and other groups within Indian society.

10 See Alison Goodrum, *The National Fabric: Fashion, Britishness, Globalization* (Oxford: Berg, 2005). Also, Juanjuan Wu, *Chinese Fashion: From Mao to Now* (Oxford: Berg, 2009). Also, Suzanne Gott and Kristyne Loughran, ed., *Contemporary African Fashion* (Indiana University Press, 2010).

11 Quote on *Verve* website www.verveonline.com.

12 www.highheelconfidential.com.

13 www.wearabout.wordpress.com.

14 Interview by Priya Kishore for *Vogue* Italy, www.*Vogue*.it.

15 Press quotes with attributions are listed here www.bombayelectric.in.

16 Sally Singer, "Hello, *Vogue* India Woman", *Vogue India*, October 2007, p.68.

17 For a more detailed discussion see Patricia Oberoi, "Feminine Identity and

National Ethos is Indian Calander Art", in *Economic and Political Weekly*, vol.25, no.17 (April 28, 1990), WS41-WS48. See also Mukulika Banerjee and Daniel Miller, *The Sari*, pp.79-87.

18 Linda Lyton, *The Sari* (London: Thames and Hudson, 1995), pp. 10-16.

19 For a fuller exploration of their phrase the 'elevated sari' and the qualities the sari embodies for the aspirational wearer see Mukulika Banerjee and Daniel Miller, *The Sari*, pp. 235-38. For a discussion of the modernization of the sari into an item of fashion, see a synopsis of the work of Dulali Nag and Naseem Khan in Jennifer Craik, *The Face of Fashion: Cultural Studies in Fashion*, pp.30-36.

20 Quote from website, www.rawmango.in.

21 *Ibid.*, Home page.

22 Series of interviews with Sanjay Garg between 2010-2012 at his studio in Delhi.

23 Asian Heritage Foundation, *Jiyo: Believe, Buy, Belong* (New Delhi: Asian Heritage Foundation, c.2009). Interview with Rajiv Sethi and visit to the studio, 15 February 2010 and 15 November 2010.

24 Interview with Swati Kalsi, by phone, March 2012.

25 *Jiyo*'s long-term legacy at the time of writing is not possible to assess.

26 Interview with David Abraham and visit to studio in Delhi, 15 November 2010 and email correspondence, 15 April 2011 and 21 January 2013.

27 Interviews with Nida Mahmood in Delhi, 18 November 2010 and Masaba Gupta in Mumbai, 26 November 2010.

28 See Mukulika Banerjee and Daniel Miller, *The Sari*, pp. 238-241.

29 Hindol Sengupta, *The Business of Indian Fashion* (Dorling Kindersley, 2009), pp. 111-113.

30 Email correspondence with David Abraham, 15 February 2013.

31 "Churi Pant", *Vogue India*, October 2007, p. 86.

32 Laila Tyabji, "Indian Textiles: Identity and Evolution", in *Handmade in India* (London: Crafts Council, 1998), pp. 42-49.

33 Series of interviews in Fedrico Rocca, *Contemporary Indian Fashion* (Damini, 2009).

34 Nasreen Askari and Rosemary Crill, *Colours of the Indus: Costumes and Textiles of Pakistan* (London: Merrell Holberton, 1996), pp. 59-63.

35 Interview with Rajesh Pratap Singh and visit to studio in Faridabad, 19 November 2010.

36 Interview with Aneeth Arora and visit to studio in Delhi, 13 November 2010 and 25 January 2012.

37 On postcard distributed at her fashion show, Spring/Summer 2010.

38 S. Dev Mahendra et al., "Economics of Handloom Weaving: A field study in Andhra Pradesh", *Economic & Political Weekly*, 24 May 2008, pp. 43-51.

39 Interview with Aneeth Arora, by phone, May 2011.

40 On postcard distributed at her fashion show, Spring/Summer 2010.

41 On postcard distributed at her fashion show, Spring/Summer 2011.

42 Jyotindra Jain, "Indian 'Folk Art': Tradition, Revival and Transformation" in *2000: Reflections on the Arts in India*, ed. Kavita Singh and Pratapatitya Pal, (Mumbai: MARG), p. 66.

43 2008 and 2011 Collections respectively.

44 On postcard distributed at her fashion show, menswear Autumn/
    Winter 2011.

45 Interview with Rajesh Pratap Singh in Faridabad, 19 November 2010.

46 For a comprehensive account of the national significance of *khadi*,
    dress, identity and the problems associated with it see Emma Tarlo,
    Clothing Matters.

47 Interview with Shenali Sema, London, April 2011.

48 As noted on his website. www.sabyasachi.com.

49 Interview in Rediff.com. www.specials.rediff.com

50 For a detailed analysis of the social and cultural aspects of weddings and the
    new middle class see Christiana Brosius, *India's Middle Class: New forms of
    Urban Leisure, Consumption and Prosperity* (New Delhi: Routledge, 2010),
    pp. 269-306.

51 Email correspondence with David Abraham, 15 February 2013.

52 Pierre Bourdieu, *Distinction: A Social Critique in the Judgement of Taste*
    (London: 1984).

53 Catriona Luke, "The Clothes Nationalist", *New Statesman*, 30 October 2008,
    www.newstatesman.com.

54 Prachi Kadam, "My Clothes are my show stoppers: Sabyasachi Mukherjee",
    DNAIndia.com, 11 March 2011, www.dnaindia.com.

55 Tim Edensor, *National identity, Popular Culture and Everyday Life* (Oxford:
    Berg, 2002), pp. 1-64.

56 Visit to studio in Delhi, 16 November 2010.

57 Here, the application of Tim Edensor's analysis of the embedded-ness of
    national identity in geographies, landscapes and the material culture of the
    everyday, could be applied to such spaces as Indian markets. Tim Edensor,
    National identity, Popular Culture and Everyday Life, pp.37-64.

58 This is demonstrated by her inclusion in Christopher Breward et al., *British
    Asian Style: Fashion and Textiles, Past & Present* (London: Victoria and Albert
    Museum, 2010).

59 "Nida Mahmood creates sparks with Machis line", in *Yahoo.com* (India), 26
    October 2010, www.nidamahmood.com.

60 *Ibid*.

61 Interview with Nida Mahmood in Delhi, 18 November 2010.

62 Warren Dotz, *Light of India: A conflation of Indian Matchbox Art* (Berkeley:
    Ten Speed Press, 2007).

63 Interviews with Rimzim Dadu and Amit Agrawal in Delhi, 17 November 2010.
    Also email correspondence with Amit Agrawal, 17 August 2011.

64 Interview with Kallol Datta in Kolkata, 22 November 2010.

65 Interview with Kallol Datta in Kolkata, 22 November 2010.

GRAPHICS IN INDIA

1 H. Kumar Vyas, *Design in India: An exhibition designed for the Festival of India
    in Britain, 1982* (Ahmedabad: National Institute of Design, 1982).

2 Interview with Rupesh Vyas, London, 13 April 2012. Also, Rupesh Vyas,
    "Information Design Interventions for Census of India" (paper presented for

Mobile Plus, International Conference on Inclusive Growth through Mobile Applications, Chennai, India, 15-17 September 2011). www.mobileplus-india.net.

3   Philip B. Meggs and Alston W. Purvis, *Meggs' History of Graphic Design* (New Jersey: John Whiley & Sons, 2012), pp. 530-572.

4   Geoffrey Caban, *World Graphic Design: Contemporary Graphics from Africa, the Far East, Latin America and the Middle East* (London: Merrell Publishers, 2004), pp.8-14.

5   Quentin Newark, *What is Graphic Design* (Switzerland: RotoVision, 2002), p. 14.

6   For general reference see Quentin Newark, (2002). Also, Rob Carter et al., *Typographic Design: Form and Communication*, (London: John Whiley & Sons, 2012). Also, Steven Heller and Mirko Llic, *Icons of Graphic Design* (London: Thames and Hudson, 2001).

7   Email communication with Priya Kishore, 24 March 2013.

8   Interview with Maithili Ahluwali by phone, 25 February 2013.

9   Visit to studio and interview with Ishan Khosla in Delhi, 27 January 2012 and interview by phone, 19 January 2013.

10 Grandmother India website: www.grandmother.in

11 Itu Chaudhuri Design website: www.icdindia.com.

12 Design Stack website: www.designstack.com.

13 Adrian Shaughnessey, "The Cult of Graphic Design", in *Looking Close: Book 5: Critical Writings on Graphic Design*, ed. Michael Beirut et al. (New York: Allworth Press, 2006), pp. 167-170.

14 Mr. Keedy, "Style is not a Four Letter Word", in Michael Beirut et al., *Looking Close: Book 5: Critical Writings on Graphic Design*, pp. 94-103.

15 Scott Minick and Jiao Ping, *Chinese Graphic Design in the Twentieth Century* (London: Thames and Hudson, 1990).

16 Divia Patel, "The Art of the Indian Film Advertising", in *Cinema India: The Art of the Hindi Film*, Rachel Dwyer and Divia Patel (London: Reaktion Press, 2002), pp. 101-183.

17 Interview with Divya Thakur by phone, 1 March 2013.

18 Quote from the exhibition panel "The Visual Language of New India", *India Now* at the Victoria and Albert Museum, Design Temple, 2007. For more information on the exhibition see www.designtemple.com.

19 Play Clan's story is on their website, Blog and Face book Page. Additional information from interview with Himanshu Dogra, Delhi, 12 March 2011. www.theplayclan.com

20 Play Clan website: www.facebook.com/ThePlayClan

21 See Play Clan website: www.theplayclan.com.

22 Interviews with Lokesh Karekar in Mumbai, 12 December 2011 and Sameer Kulavoor, 13 December 2011.

23 See Pentagram website: www.pentagram.in

24 Catalogue on their website: www.grandmother.in.

25 Sameer Kulavoor, "At Filter in Mumbai", *Mumbai Boss,* 12 March 2012. www.theindialube.com.

26 Interview with V. Sunil by phone, 26 March 2013

27 Press release available on their website: www.motherlandmagazine.com.

28 Quoted in Partha Mitter, *Much Maligned Monsters: A History of European Reactions to Indian Art* (Oxford: Clarendon Press, 1977), p. 230.

29 Alice Twemlow, "The Decriminalisation of Ornament", *Eye Magazine*, no.58, vol.15, Winter 2005.

30 Brijesh Patel, "Indian Mag Culture: Motherland", Parchai website: www.parchai.com.

31 Ramachandran Guha on Seminar Magazine Facebook page: www.facebook.com.

32 Sesh Design website: www.seshdesign.com.

33 Email correspondence with Akila Seshasayee, 19 March 2013.

34 Email correspondence with Akila Seshasayee, 1 Novermber 2011.

35 A fuller description of the cover design given by Akila Seshasayee via email correspondence, 19 March 2013, is as follows: 'The cover is a representation of the chakravyuha, the disc like military formation devised by dronacharya in the battle of Kurukshetra which required special knowledge to penetrate. In the absence of Arjuna and Pradyumna, Abhimanyu volunteer to infiltrate it inspite of having partial knowledge of entry, but not exit – thereby depicting enduring capability and bravery of humans to fight for dharma in the face of chaos and uncertainty. In this case, the 'chakravyuha disc' also resembles tree rings which denote age.'

36 Interview with Rajesh Dahiya by phone, 20 March 2013.

37 Codesign, *Dekho: Conversations on Design in India 2012* (India: Codesign, 2012), p.5.

38 Christian Morgenstern, *In the Land of Punctuation* (Chennai: Tara Books, 2009). See also Rathna Ramanathan's explanation of her working process on her website: www.m9design.com.

39 Samhita Arni and Moyna Chitrakar, *Sita's Ramayana* (Chennai: Tara Books, 2011) and Moyna Chitrakar and Joydeb Chitrakar, *Tsunami* (Chennai: Tara Books, 2009).

40 Rathna Ramanathan, "Picturing Words: Associative Typography and the Picture Book", (paper presented at the Typography workshop held at the Industrial Design Centre at the India Institute of Technology, Mumbai, India, 1-3 March 2012).

41 See interview with Gita Wolf in the Seagull School of Publishing Blog, 10 August 2012, www.theseagullschool.wordpress.com.

42 For an overview of the interaction of artist and designer see V. Geetha, *Sita's Ramayana: The Many Lives of a Text* on Tara Books Blog, 5 December 2011, www.tarabooks.com.

43 Durgabai, Vyam et al., *Bhimayana: Experiences of Untouchability* (Delhi: Navayana Press, 2011). Interview with S. Anand in Delhi, 4 February 2012. See also, Subuhi Jiwani, "The Real Super-heroes", *Art India*, vol XVI Issue IV, (2012): 48-51. Also, Rama Lakshmi, "Indian graphic artists draw outside the box for nonfiction 'Bhimayan'," *The Washington Post*, 19 August 2010, www.washingtonpost.com.

44 Durgabai, Vyam et al., *Bhimayana: Experiences of Untouchability*, pp. 96-104.

45 *Ibid.*, p. 100

46 Piers Carey, "From the Outside In: A Place for Indigenous Graphic Traditions in Contemporary South African Graphic Design", *Design Issues*, vol. 27, no.1 (2011): 55-62.

47 For example, Keith Lovegrove, *Graphicswallah: Graphics in India*, (London: Laurence King, 2003). Also, Barry Dawson, *Street Graphics India*, (London:

Thames and Hudson, 1999). Also, Luigi Giannuzzi, ed. Cock: *Indian Firework Art* (London: Westzone Publishing, 2000).

48 Shahid Datawala, *Matchbook: Indian Matchbox Labels* (Chennai: Tara Books, 2007). Also Kajri Jain, *Gods in the Bazaar: The Economies of Indian Calendar Art* (Duke University Press, 2007). Meena Kadri, "Sign Wallahs: An exploration of the Indian Streetscape", *Lab Magazine*, 2 (2008). Gauri Mathur, "Signboards as Mirrors of Cultural Change", *Design Issues*, vol.21, no.4, (2005): 78-92. Ken Botnick and Ira Raja, "Subtle Technology: The Design Innovation of Indian Artisanship", *Design Issues*, vol.27, no.4, (2011): 43-55.

49 Anand Tharaney, "The CR Taxi," *Creative Review*, 24 March 2009, www.creativereview.co.uk. See also www.aresearchdocument.blogspot.co.uk.

50 Malaika Byng, "India Typeface by Geeta Alok and Henrik Kubel," Wallpaper*, 11 May 2011, www.wallpaper.com.

51 Handpainted Type website: www.handpaintedtype.com

52 Interview with Hanif Kureshi in Delhi, 28 January 2012.

53 Interview with Rathna Ramanathan by phone, 2 March 2013. See also Rathna Ramanathan, "Town Type. The hidden typographers of Tamil Nadu", (paper presented at Friends of St Bride Printing Library second annual conference, St Bride Institute, London, 20-21 October 2003), www.stbride.org.

INTERIORS IN INDIA

1   Henry Wilson, *India Contemporary* (London: Thames and Hudson, 2007). Angelika Taschen, ed. *Indian Interiors* (Taschen, 2009).

2   *India Design* (Cologne: Daab, 2004).

3   Muktirajsinhji Chauhan and Kamalika Bose, *A History of Interior Design in India, vol 1: Ahmedabad* (Ahmedabad: CEPT University, 2007).

4   Interview with Ayush and Gitanjali Kasliwal in Jaipur, 16 March 2011.

5   Examples in Muktirajsinhji Chauhan and Kamalika Bose, *A History of Interior Design in India*, pp.228-233.

6   AKFD Press release, *AKFD: An Indian Design Saga in the Making*, no date.

7   Ayush Kasliwal and Geetanjali Kasliwal, *Crafts of Sultana*, unpublished booklet.

8   *Ibid*.

9   Email conversation with Ayush Kasliwal, 7 May 2011.

10 Interview with Vikram Goyal in London, May 2011.

11 Email exchange with Vikram Goyal, 8 June 2011.

12 Ulf Hannerz and Orvar Löfgren, 'The Nation in the Global Village', *Cultural Studies*, 8(2):198-207, as quoted in Alison Goodrum, *The National Fabric* (Oxford: Berg, 2005), p. 69.

13 AKFD Press release, *AKFD: An Indian Design Saga in the Making*, no date.

14 Viya Home and Odegard association took place in 2010. www.viyahome.com

15 Marissa Brunfman, "Jewels of Wisdon: Good Earth founder, Anita Lal's Story of Passion and Perseverance," *Huffington Post.Com*, 18 June 2012, www.huffingtonpost.com.

16 Goodearth website: www.goodearth.in.

17 Visit to Studio and interview with Gunjan Gupta in Delhi, 15 March 2011.

18 Interviews with Sahil Bagga and Sarthak Sengupta in Delhi, 15 March 2011.

19 Victor Papanek, *Design for the Real World* (London: Thames and Husdon, 1972), and, E.F. Schumacher, *Small is Beautiful: A study of Economics as if People Mattered* (Blond and Briggs, 1973).

20 Richard Buchanan, "Wicked Problems in Design Thinking", *Design Issues*, vol.8, no.2 (1991): 5-21.

21 Tim Brown, *Change by Design* (New York: Harper Collins, 2009) and, Tom Kelly, *The Art of Innovation* (London: Profile Books, 2004).

22 Simon Keane-Cowell, "Bamboo: the design material that keeps on giving", Architonic, online article, 2010, www.architonic.com.

23 For an overview of M.P. Ranjan's story see M.P. Ranjan, "Raindrops & Footprints: Reflections on Design enabled development models for India", (Keynote presentation at FISCAR, at Alton University, Helsinki, 23-25 May 2010).

24 The workshops and collections produced are as follows: The Tripura Collection of 1986, the UNDP collection of 1999, the Bamboo Boards collection of 2000 and the BCDI collection, 2002-2004.

25 *Cube Stool & Seating Systems, Case Study*, NID Ahmedabad and Development Commissioner of Handicrafts Govt. India. For summary presentation see NID Bamboo Products in Indian Handicrafts and Gift Fair, Pragati Madhan, New Delhi, 13–16 October 2002, NID, Ahmedabad.

26 M.P. Ranjan, *Katlamaro Chalo: A Design for Development Strategy* (Ahmedabad: Centre for Bamboo Initiatives at the National Institute of Design).

27 Andrea Noronha, *Bamboo Product Development for Tripura Bamboo Mission*, Diploma Project, Industrial Design Faculty (Furniture and Interior Design) Ahmedabad, National Institute of Design, 2009.

28 Interview with Andrea Noronha, 21 March 2011. Email exchange 16 June 2011.

29 Interview with Rebecca Reubens in Ahmedabad, 21 March 2011. See also articles Rebecca Reubens, *Bamboo in Contemporary Sustainable Art Design*, INBAR, working paper no.60. Also, Rebecca Reubens, *Bamboo: From Green Design to Sustainable Design* (Antwerp: Promilla, 2012).

30 Visit to studio and interview with Sanjeev Sangaru in Bangalore, 19 December 2011.

31 Sanjeev Sangaru website: www.sangaru.com

32 Marcus Fairs, "Doshi Levien for Moroso/2", *Dezeen*, Online Magazine, 24 April 2007, www.dezeen.com. Also, "Cultural Nomad" in *Design Indaba Magazine*, 2005, pp.32-39.

33 A number of articles re-enforce the same message: Dhanu Kandappah, "doshi levien: designing a new country", *IFJ*, Sept-Oct 2008, pp.38-43. Also, Kavita Rayirath, "Doshi Levien", *Indian by Design* Blog, 23 June 2009, www. indianbydesign.wordpress.com. See also Jonathan Levien, "Best of Both Worlds," *Damn* 12 (2007): 66-69, www.doshilevien.com.

34 Detailed account of the charpoy see Marcus Fairs, "Doshi Levien for Moroso/2", www.dezeen.com.

35 Jonathan Levien, "Best of Both Worlds".

36 Dhanu Kandappah, "doshi levien: designing a new country," p.42. On craft, layering and eurocentricity see Nadine Botha, "1+1 makes 3," in Design

Indaba website, 1 November 2007, www.designindaba.com/news/ 11-makes-3.

37 Visit to studio and interview with Satyendra Pakhalé, 27 May 2011. For process see: Jana Szita, "Satyendra Pakhalé: Nomadic design", in *Amsterdam Index*, 2007, pp. 53-55. Also, Jana Szita, "Pure and Symbol", *Dwell*, vol.7, no.3 (2007): pp. 114-119.

38 Dhanu Kandappah, "doshi levien: designing a new country," p.39.

39 Nipa Doshi, "Made for India," *Wallpaper**, March 2006, p. 78, www.doshilevien.com.

40 The Lebua Hotels and Resorts are a luxury brand specializing in hotel, restaurant and bar management. They took over management of Devi Garh and Devi Ratn in January 2013.

41 www.openbuildings.com.

42 Series of interviews with Rajiv Saini held in Mumbai between 2009-2012.

43 Visit to studio and interviews with Bijou Jain in Alibag, 24 March 2011 and 31 January 2012. For overviews see Kasi A. Asraf, ed. Made in India, *Architectural Digest*, vol. 77 no.6. (2007): 36-41.

44 Cyril Veillon, *Work- Place: Studio Mumbai*, Éditions Archizoom (Lausanne, Switzerland, 2011), p.84.

45 *Ibid.,* for examples.

46 *Ibid.,* for Studio Mumbai's work philosophy, p.26.

47 Interview with Kapil Gupta in Mumbai, 16 December 2011.

48 Quote from website www.serie.co.uk. See also, Rahul Mehrotra, Architecture in India since 1990 (Germany, Hatje Cantz, 2011), pp. 113-115.

49 Interview with Ayaz Basrai in Mumbai, 14 December 2011.

BIBLIOGRAPHY

Ahmedabad: National Institute of Design. *Cube Stool & Seating Systems, Case Study.* c.2002.

Ahmedabad: National Institute of Design. *National Design Policy.* 2007.

Arni, Samhita, and Moyna Chitrakar. *Sita's Ramayana.* Chennai: Tara Books, 2011.

Arts, Wil. Introduction to *Through a Glass Darkly, Blurred Images of Cultural Tradition and Modernity over distance and time,* pp.1-9. Netherlands: Brill, 2000.

Ashraf, Kazi K. and James Belluardo ed. *An Architecture of Independence.* New York: The Architectural League of New York, 1998.

Asian Heritage Foundation. *Jiyo: Believe, Buy, Belong.* New Delhi: Asian Heritage Foundation, c.2009.

Askari, Nasreen, and Rosemary Crill. *Colours of the Indus: Costumes and Textiles of Pakistan.* London: Merrell Holberton, 1996.

Athavankar, Uday. "Design in Search of Roots: An Indian Experience", *Design Issues,* vol.18, no.3, (2002): 43-57.

Balram, Singanapali. *Thinking Design.* Ahmedabad: National Institute of Design, 1998.

Banerjee, Mukulika, and Daniel Miller. *The Sari.* Oxford: Berg, 2003.

Bhowmick, Subrata. "How it all Began", *Pool Magazine* 6 (2010): 14.

Boroian, Michael, and Alix de Poix. *Indian by Design: The Pursuit of Luxury and Fashion.* Singapore: John Wiley & Sons, 2010.

Botnick, Ken, and Ira Raja. "Subtle Technology: The Design Innovation of Indian Artisanship", *Design Issues,* vol.27, no.4, (2011): 43-55.

Botha, Nadine. "1+1 makes 3", in Design Indaba website, 1 November 2007. www.designindaba.com.

Bourdieu, Pierre. *Distinction: A Social Critique in the Judgement of Taste.* London: 1984.

Breward, Christopher. ed. *British Asian Style: Fashion and Textiles, Past & Present.* London: Victoria and Albert Museum, 2010.

Brosius, Christiana. *India's Middle Class: New forms of Urban Leisure, Consumption and Prosperity.* New Delhi: Routledge, 2010.

Buchanan, Richard. "Wicked Problems in Design Thinking", *Design Issues,* vol.8, no.2 (1991): 5-21.

Byng, Malaika. "India Typeface by Geeta Alok and Henrik Kubel", *Wallpaper*,* 11 May 2011, www.wallpaper.com.

Caban, Geoffrey. *World Graphic Design: Contemporary Graphics from Africa, the Far East, Latin America and the Middle East.* London: Merrell Publishers, 2004.

Carey, Piers. "From the Outside In: A Place for Indigenous Graphic Traditions in Contemporary South African Graphic Design", *Design Issues,* vol. 27, no.1 (2011): 55-62.

Carter, Rob., Ben Day, and Philip B. Meggs. *Typographic Design: Form and Communication.* London: John Whiley & Sons, 2012.

Castelino, Meher. *Fashion Kaleidoscope*. India: Rupa Publishing, 1994.

Chatterjee, Ashoke. "Design in India: The Experience of Transition", *Design Issues*, vol.21, no.4 (2005): 4-10.

Chaudhuri, Supriya. *Modernisms in India*. Oxford University Press, Uncorrected proof, p.954, www.academia.edu.

Chauhan, Muktirajsinhji, and Kamalika Bose. *A History of Interior Design in India, vol 1: Ahmedabad*. Ahmedabad: CEPT University, 2007.

Chitrakar, Moyna, and Joydeb Chitrakar. *Tsunami*. Chennai: Tara Books, 2009.

Cologne: Daab, *India Design*, 2004.

Codesign, *Dekho: Conversations on Design in India 2012*. India: Codesign, 2012.

Craik, Jennifer. *The Face of Fashion: Cultural Studies in Fashion*. London: Routledge, 1993.

Datawala, Shahid. *Matchbook: Indian Matchbox Labels*. Chennai: Tara Books, 2007.

Dawson, Barry. *Street Graphics India*. London: Thames and Hudson, 1999.

Doshi, Nipa. "Made for India", *Wallpaper**, March 2006, p.78, www.doshilevien.com.

Dotz, Warren. *Light of India: A conflation of Indian Matchbox Art*. Berkeley: Ten Speed Press, 2007.

Eames, Charles, and Ray Eames, *The India Report*. Ahmedabad: National Institute of Design. No date.

Edensor, Tim. *National identity, Popular Culture and Everyday Life*. Oxford: Berg, 2002.

Fairs, Marcus. "Doshi Levien for Moroso/2", www.dezeen.com.

Gaonkar, Dilip. "On Alternative Modernities", *Public Culture*, vol 11, no.1 (1999) pp. 1- 18.

Ganesh, Kamala, and Usha Thakkar, eds. *Culture and the Making of Identity in Contemporary India*. New Delhi: Sage, 2005.

Ghurye, G.S. *Indian Costume*. Bombay: Popular Book Depot, 1951.

Giannuzzi, Luigi, ed. Cock. *Indian Firework Art*. London: Westzone Publishing, 2000.

Goetz, Hermann. "The Calico Museum of Textiles at Ahmedabad", *Marg*, vol.3, no.4 (1949): 58.

Goodrum, Alison. *The National Fabric: Fashion, Britishness and Globalization*. London: Berg, 2005.

Gott, Suzanne, and Kristyne Loughran, ed. *Contemporary African Fashion*. Indiana University Press, 2010.

Heller, Steven, and Mirko Llic. *Icons of Graphic Design*. London: Thames and Hudson, 2001.

Hobsbawm, Eric, and Terence Ranger, eds. *The Invention of Tradition*. Cambridge: Cambridge University Press, 1983.

Hopper, Paul. *Understanding Cultural Globalization*. USA: Malden, 2011.

Jain, Kajri. *Gods in the Bazaar: The Economies of Indian Calendar Art*. Duke University Press, 2007.

Jani, Abu, and Sandeep Khosla. *India Fantastique*. London: Thames and Hudson, 2012.

Jain, Jyotindra. "Indian 'Folk Art': Tradition, Revival and Transformation", in *2000: Reflections on The Arts of India*, edited by Pratapaditya Pal, p.66. Mumbai: Marg Publications, 2000.

Jayakar, Papul. Editorial to *Homage to Handloom*, *Marg*, vol.15. no.4 (1962): 3.

Jiwani, Subuhi. "The Real Super-heroes", *Art India*, vol XVI Issue IV, (2012): 48-51.

Julier, Guy. *The Culture of Design*. London: Sage Publications, 2008.

Julier, Guy. "Locating Design Cultures". Paper presented at the Premsela Design Cultures symposium, UV Amsterdam, 25 May 2011.

Kadri, Meena. "Sign Wallahs: An exploration of the Indian Streetscape", *Lab Magazine*, 2 (2008).

Kandappah, Dhanu. "Doshi Levien: Designing a New Country", *IFJ*, Sept-Oct 2008, pp. 38-43.

Kawamura, Yuniya. *Fashion-ology: An introduction to Fashion studies*. Oxford: Berg, 2005.

Keane-Cowell, Simon. "Bamboo: the design material that keeps on giving". *Architonic*, online article, 2010, www.architonic.com.

Khan, Naseem. "Asian Women's Dress: from Burqah to Bloggs – changing clothes for changing times", in *Chic Thrill*, edited by Juliet Ash and Elizabeth Wilson, pp. 61-74. London: Pandora Press, 1992.

Khilnani, Sunil. *The Idea of India*. London: Hamilton Hamish, 1997.

Kulavoor, Sameer. "At Filter in Mumbai", in *Mumbai Boss*, 12 March 2012. www.theindiatube.com.

Kumar, Nirmalya. *India's Global Powerhouses*. Harvard Business Press, 2009.

Kumar, Ritu. *Costumes and Textiles of Royal India*. London: Christie's books, 1999.

Lakshmi, Rama. "Indian graphic artists draw outside the box for nonfiction 'Bhimayan'", *The Washington Post*, 19 August 2010, www.washingtonpost.com.

Levien, Jonathan. "Best of Both Worlds", *Damn* 12 (2007): 66-69, www.doshilevien.com.

Lovegrove, Keith. *Graphicswallah: Graphics in India*. London: Laurence King, 2003.

Lyton, Linda. *The Sari*. London: Thames and Hudson, 1995.

Luke, Catriona. "The Clothes Nationalist", in *New Statesman*, 30 October 2008, www.newstatesman.com.

Madhok, Ruchita. "The Rise of the Design Event", in online magazine *Perch*, 7 August 2012, www.perchontheweb.com.

Margolin, Victor. "A History of Design and the History of the World", *Journal of Design History*, vol. 18, no. 3, (2005), pp. 235-243.

Mathur, Gauri. "Signboards as Mirrors of Cultural Change", *Design Issues*, vol.21, no.4, (2005): 78-92.

Mathur, Saloni. *India by Design: Colonial History and Cultural Display*. Berkeley: University of Californiam, 2007.

Mathur, Saloni. "Charles and Ray Eames in India", *Art Journal*, vol.70. no.1 (2011): 34-53.

Mr. Keedy. "Style is not a Four Letter Word", in *Looking Close: Book 5: Critical Writings on Graphic Design*, edited by Michael Beirut, William Drenttel & Steven Heller, pp. 94-103. New York: Allworth Press, 2006.

Meggs, Philip B., and Alston W. Purvis. *Meggs' History of Graphic Design*. New Jersey: John Whiley & Sons, 2012.

Mehrotra, Rahul. *Architecture in India since 1990*. Germany: Hatje Cantz, 2011.

Minick, Scott, and Jiao Ping. *Chinese Graphic Design in the Twentieth Century*. London: Thames and Hudson, 1990.

Mitter, Partha. *Much Maligned Monsters: A History of European Reactions to Indian Art*. Oxford: Clarendon Press, 1977.

McGowan, Abigail. *Crafting the Nation in Colonial India*. New York: Palgrave MacMillian, 2009.

Morgenstern, Christian. *In the Land of Punctuation*. Chennai: Tara Books, 2009.

Nag, Dulali. "Fashion, gender and the Bengali middle class", *Public Culture*, vol.3, no.2 (1991): 93-112.

Newark, Quentin. *What is Graphic Design*, Switzerland: RotoVision, 2002.

Noronha, Andrea. "Bamboo Product Development for Tripura Bamboo Mission", Diploma Project, Industrial Design Faculty (Furniture and Interior Design) Ahmedabad, National Institute of Design, 2009.

Oberoi, Patricia. "Feminine Identity and National Ethos is Indian Calander Art", in *Economic and Political Weekly*, vol.25, no.17 (28 April 1990), WS41-WS48.

Papanek, Victor. *Design for the Real World*. London: Thames and Husdon, 1972.

Patel, Divia. "The Art of the Indian Film Advertising", in *Cinema India: The Art of the Hindi Film*, by Rachel Dwyer and Divia Patel, pp. 101-183. London: Reaktion Press, 2002.

Prahlad, C.K. *Fortune at the Bottom of the Pyramid*. New Jersey: Pearson Education, 2005.

Rajdou, Navi, Jaideep Prabhu and Simone Ahuja. *Jugaard Innovation*. San Francisco: Jossey-Bass, 2010.

Ramanathan, Rathna. "Town Type. The hidden typographers of Tamil Nadu", Paper presented at Friends of St Bride Printing Library second annual conference, St Bride Institute, London, 20-21 October 2003.

Ramanathan, Rathna. "Picturing Words: Associative Typography and the Picture Book". Paper presented at the Typography workshop held at the Industrial Design Centre at the India Institute of Technology, Mumbai, India, 1-3 March 2012.

Ranjan, M.P. "Raindrops & Footprints: Reflections on Design enabled development models for India". Keynote presentation at FISCAR, at Alton University, Helsinki, 23-25 May 2010.

Ranjan, M.P. *Katlamaro Chalo: A Design for Development Strategy*. Ahmedabad: Centre for Bamboo Initiatives at the National Institute of Design, 2005.

Rayirath, Kavita. "Doshi Levien", *Indian by Design* Blog, 23 June 2009, www.indianbydesign.wordpress.com.

Reubens, Rebecca. *Bamboo in Contemporary Sustainable Art Design*, INBAR, working paper no.60.

Reubens, Rebecca. *Bamboo: From Green Design to Sustainable Design*. Antwerp: Promilla, 2012.

Rocca, Fedric. *Contemporary Indian Fashion*. Damini, 2009.

S. Mahendra Dev, S. Galab, P. Prudhvikar Reddy and Soymya Vinayan. "Economics of Handloom Weaving: A field study in Andhra Pradesh", *Economic & Political Weekly*, 24 May 2008, pp. 43-51.

Sen, Amartya. The Argumentative Indian. India· Penguin, 2005.

Sengupta, Hindol. *The Business of Indian Fashion*. Dorling Kindersley, 2009.

Shaughnessey, Adrian. "The Cult of Graphic Design", in *Looking Close: Book 5: Critical Writings on Graphic Design*, edited by Michael Beirut, William Drenttel & Steven Heller, pp. 167-170. New York: Allworth Press, 2006.

Sharma, L.K., and Shobit Arya. *The India Idea*. Wisdom Tree, 2011.

Singer, Sally. "Hello, *Vogue* India Woman", *Vogue India*, October 2007, p. 68.

Singh, Kavita. "Mulk Raj Anand: A Visionary Aesthete", in *2000: Reflections on The Arts of India*, edited by Pratapaditya Pal, p. 20. Mumbai: Marg Publications 2000.

Singh, Radhika, *The Fabric of Our Lives: The Story of FabIndia*. India: Penguin, 2010.

Szita, Jana. "Satyendra Pakhalé: Nomadic design", in *Amsterdam Index*, 2007, pp. 53-55.

Szita, Jana. "Pure and Symbol", in *Dwell*, vol.7, no.3 (2007): pp. 114-119.

Subramanyan, K.G. "Contemporary Design developments in Handlooms", *Marg*, vol.15, no.4 (1962): 42.

Taschen, Angelika. ed. *Indian Interiors*. Taschen, 2009.

Tarlo, Emma. *Clothing Matters*. London: C. Hurst & Co., 1996.

Tharaney, Anand, "The CR Taxi", *Creative Review*, 24 March 2009.

Twemlow, Alice. "The Decriminalisation of Ornament", in *Eye Magazine*, no.58, vol.15, Winter 2005.

Tyabji, Laila. "Indian Textiles: Identity and Evolution", in *Handmade in India*, pp. 42-49. London: Crafts Council, 1998.

Varma, Pavan K. *Being Indian*. India: Penguin, 2004.

Vasudev, Shefalee. *Powder Room: The Untold Story of Indian Fashion*. India: Random House, 2012.

Veillon, Cyril. *Work-Place: Studio Mumbai*, Éditions Archizoom. Lausanne, Switzerland, 2011.

Vyam, Durgabai, Subhash Vyam, Srividya Natarajan and S. Anand. *Bhimayana: Experiences of Untouchability*. Delhi: Navayana Press, 2011.

Vyas, H. Kumar. *Design in India: An Exhibition designed for the Festival of India in Britain, 1982*. Ahmedabad: National Institute of Design, 1982.

Vyas, H. Kumar. *Design: The Indian Context*. Ahmedabad: National Institute of Design, 2000.

Vyas, Rupesh. "Information Design Interventions for Census of India". Paper presented for Mobile Plus, International Conference on Inclusive Growth through Mobile Applications, Chennai, India, 15-17 September 2011, www. mobileplus-india.net

Wilson, Henry. *India Contemporary*. London: Thames and Hudson, 2007.

Wu, Juanjuan. *Chinese Fashion: From Mao to Now*. Oxford: Berg, 2009.

WEBSITES

www.openbuildings.com
www.serie.co.uk
www.verveonline.com
www.handpaintedtype.com
www.sabyasachi.com
www.m9design.com
www.seshdesign.com
www.grandmother.in
www.icdindia.com
www.designstack.com
www.theplayclan.com

© Victoria and Albert Museum, London.
Published in India by Roli Books
in association with V&A Publishing, London.
M-75, Greater Kailash II Market, New Delhi-110 048, India
Ph: ++91-11-4068 2000; Fax: ++91-11-2921 7185
E-mail: info@rolibooks.com, Website: www.rolibooks.com

ISBN: 978-81-7436-975-8

Editors: Priya Kapoor, Neelam Narula
Photo-editor: Saloni Vaid
Design and layout: Bonita Vaz-Shimray, Naresh L. Mondal
Pre-press: Jyoti Dey
Production: Naresh Nigam and Shaji Sahadevan

Printed and bound in China

INDIA Contemporary Design